Kansas City Royals 2020

A Baseball Companion

Edited by R.J. Anderson, Craig Goldstein and Bret Sayre

Baseball Prospectus

Craig Brown, Steven Goldman and David Pease, Consultant Editors
Robert Au, Harry Pavlidis and Amy Pircher, Statistics Editors

Copyright © 2020 by DIY Baseball, LLC.
All rights reserved

This book or any part thereof may not be reproduced or transmitted in any form or by any means, electronic or mechanical, including photocopying, recording, or by any information storage and retrieval system, without permission in writing from the publisher.

Limit of Liability/Disclaimer of Warranty: While the publisher and the author have used their best efforts in preparing this book, they make no representations or warranties with respect to the accuracy or completeness of the contents of this book and specifically disclaim any implied warranties of merchantability or fitness for a particular purpose. No warranty may be created or extended by sales representatives or written sales materials. The advice and strategies contained herein may not be suitable for your situation. You should consult with a professional where appropriate. Neither the publisher nor the author shall be liable for any loss of profit or any other commercial damages, including but not limited to special, incidental, consequential, or other damages.

Library of Congress Cataloging-in-Publication Data:
paperback
ISBN-13: 978-1-949332-76-6

Project Credits
Cover Design: Michael Byzewski at Aesthetic Apparatus
Interior Design and Production: Jeff Pease, Dave Pease
Layout: Jeff Pease, Dave Pease

Baseball icon courtesy of Uberux, from https://www.shareicon.net/author/uberux

Ballpark diagram courtesy of Lou Spirito/THIRTY81 Project, https://thirty81project.com/

Manufactured in the United States of America
10 9 8 7 6 5 4 3 2 1

Table of Contents

Statistical Introduction v

Part 1: Team Analysis

Kansas City Royals: Where Are You Going, Where Have You Been? 3
    Lucas Apostoleris, Ben Spanier and Matthew Trueblood

Performance Graphs 7

2019 Team Performance 8

2020 Team Projections 9

Team Personnel 10

Kauffman Stadium Stats 11

Royals Team Analysis 13

Part 2: Player Analysis

Royals Player Analysis 20

Royals Prospects 101

Part 3: Featured Articles

The Baseball Is Juiced (Again) 117
    Robert Arthur

The Moral Hazard of Playing It Safe 121
    Craig Goldstein

Index of Names 127

Statistical Introduction

Sports are, fundamentally, a blend of athletic endeavor and storytelling. Baseball, like any other sport, tells its stories in so many ways: in the arc of a game from the stands or a season from the box scores, in photos, or even in numbers. At Baseball Prospectus, we understand that statistics don't replace observation or any of baseball's stories, but complement everything else that makes the game so much fun.

What stats help us with is with patterns and precision, variance and value. This book can help you learn things you may not see from watching a game or hundred, whether it's the path of a career over time or the breadth of the entire MLB. We'd also never ask you to choose between our numbers and the experience of viewing a game from the cheap seats or the comfort of your home; our publication combines running the numbers with observations and wisdom from some of the brightest minds we can find. But if you *do* want to learn more about the numbers beyond what's on the backs of player jerseys, let us help explain.

Offense

We've revised our methodology for determining batting value. Long-time readers of the book will notice that we've retired True Average in favor of a new metric: Deserved Runs Created Plus (DRC+). Developed by Jonathan Judge and our stats team, this statistic measures everything a player does at the plate–reaching base, hitting for power, making outs, and moving runners over–and puts it on a scale where 100 equals league-average performance. A DRC+ of 150 is terrific, a DRC+ of 100 is average and a DRC+ of 75 means you better be an excellent defender.

DRC+ also does a better job than any of our previous metrics in taking contextual factors into account. The model adjusts for how the park affects performance, but also for things like the talent of the opposing pitcher, value of different types of batted-ball events, league, temperature and other factors. It's able to describe a player's expected offensive contribution than any other statistic we've found over the years, and also does a better job of predicting future performance as well.

There's a lot more to DRC+'s story, and you can read all about it in greater depth near the end of this book.

The other aspect of run-scoring is baserunning, which we quantify using Baserunning Runs. BRR not only records the value of stolen bases (or getting caught in the act), but also accounts for all the stuff that doesn't show up on the back of a baseball card: a runner's ability to go first to third on a single, or advance on a fly ball.

Defense

Where offensive value is *relatively* easy to identify and understand, defensive value is...not. Over the past dozen years, the sabermetric community has focused mostly on stats based on zone data: a real-live human person records the type of batted ball and estimated landing location, and models are created that give expected outs. From there, you can compare fielders' actual outs to those expected ones. Simple, right?

Unfortunately, zone data has two major issues. First, zone data is recorded by commercial data providers who keep the raw data private unless you pay for it. (All the statistics we build in this book and on our website use public data as inputs.) That hurts our ability to test assumptions or duplicate results. Second, over the years it has become apparent that there's quite a bit of "noise" in zone-based fielding analysis. Sometimes the conclusions drawn from zone data don't hold up to scrutiny, and sometimes the different data provided by different providers don't look anything alike, giving wildly different results. Sometimes the hard-working professional stringers or scorers might unknowingly inflict unconscious bias into the mix: for example good fielders will often be credited with more expected outs despite the data, and ballparks with high press boxes tend to score more line drives than ones with a lower press box.

Enter our Fielding Runs Above Average (FRAA). For most positions, FRAA is built from play-by-play data, which allows us to avoid the subjectivity found in many other fielding metrics. The idea is this: count how many fielding plays are made by a given player and compare that to expected plays for an average fielder at their position (based on pitcher ground ball tendencies and batter handedness). Then we adjust for park and base-out situations.

When it comes to catchers, our methodology is a little different thanks to the laundry list of responsibilities they're tasked with beyond just, well, catching and throwing the ball. By now you've probably heard about "framing" or the art of making umpires more likely to call balls outside the strike zone for strikes. To put this into one tidy number, we incorporate pitch tracking data (for the years it exists) and adjust for important factors like pitcher, umpire, batter and home-field advantage using a mixed-model approach. This grants us a number for how many strikes the catcher is personally adding to (or subtracting from) his pitchers' performance...which we then convert to runs added or lost using linear weights.

Framing is one of the biggest parts of determining catcher value, but we also take into account blocking balls from going past, whether a scorer deems it a passed ball or a wild pitch. We use a similar approach—one that really benefits from the pitch tracking data that tells us what ends up in the dirt and what doesn't. We also include a catcher's ability to prevent stolen bases and how well they field balls in play, and *finally* we come up with our FRAA for catchers.

Pitching

Both pitching and fielding make up the half of baseball that isn't run scoring: run prevention. Separating pitching from fielding is a tough task, and most recent pitching analysis has branched off from Voros McCracken's famous (and controversial) statement, "There is little if any difference among major-league pitchers in their ability to prevent hits on balls hit in the field of play." The research of the analytic community has validated this to some extent, and there are a host of "defense-independent" pitching measures that have been developed to try and extract the effect of the defense behind a hurler from the pitcher's work.

Our solution to this quandary is Deserved Run Average (DRA), our core pitching metric. DRA looks like earned run average (ERA), the tried-and-true pitching stat you've seen on every baseball broadcast or box score from the past century, but it's very different. To start, DRA takes an event-by-event look at what the pitchers does, and adjusts the value of that event based on different environmental factors like park, batter, catcher, umpire, base-out situation, run differential, inning, defense, home field advantage, pitcher role and temperature. That mixed model gives us a pitcher's expected contribution, similar to what we do for our DRC+ model for hitters and FRAA model for catchers. (Oh, and we also consider the pitcher's effect on basestealing and on balls getting past the catcher.)

It's important to note that DRA is set to the scale of runs allowed per nine innings (RA9) instead of ERA, which makes DRA's scale slightly higher than ERA's. The reason for this is because ERA tends to overrate three types of pitchers:

1. Pitchers who play in parks where scorers hand out more errors. Official scorers differ significantly in the frequency at which they assign errors to fielders.
2. Ground-ball pitchers, because a substantial proportion of errors occur on groundballs.
3. Pitchers who aren't very good. Better pitchers often allow fewer unearned runs than bad pitchers, because good pitchers tend to find ways to get out of jams.

Kansas City Royals 2020

Since the last time you picked up an edition of this book, we've also made a few minor changes to DRA to make it better. Recent research into "tunneling"—the act of throwing consecutive pitches that appear similar from a batter's point of view until after the swing decision point–data has given us a new contextual factor to account for in DRA: plate distance. This refers to the distance between successive pitches as they approach the plate, and while it has a smaller effect than factors like velocity or whiff rate, it still can help explain pitcher strikeout rate in our model.

New Pitching Metrics for 2020

We're including a few "new" pitching metrics in the book for the 2020 edition, though unlike last year, these numbers may be a little bit more familiar to those of you who have spent some time investigating baseball statistics.

Fastball Percentage

Our fastball percentage (FB%) statistic measures how frequently a pitcher throws a pitch classified as a "fastball," measured as a percentage of overall pitches thrown. We qualify three types of fastballs:

1. The traditional four-seam fastball;
2. The two-seam fastball or sinker;
3. "Hard cutters," which are pitches that have the movement profile of a cut fastball and are used as the pitcher's primary offering or in place of a more traditional fastball.

For example, a pitcher with a FB% of 67 throws any combination of these three pitches about two-thirds of the time.

Whiff Rate

Everybody loves a swing and a miss, and whiff rate (WHF) measures how frequently pitchers induce a swinging strike. To calculate WHF, we add up all the pitches thrown that ended with a swinging strike, then divide that number by a pitcher's total pitches thrown. Most often, high whiff rates correlate with high strikeout rates (and overall effective pitcher performance).

Called Strike Probability

Called Strike Probability (CSP) is a number that represents the likelihood that all of a pitcher's pitches will be called a strike while controlling for location, pitcher and batter handedness, umpire and count. Here's how it works: on each pitch, our model determines how many times (out of 100) that a similar pitch was called for a strike given those factors mentioned above, and when normalized for each batter's strike zone. Then we average the CSP for all pitches thrown by a pitcher in a season, and that gives us the yearly CSP percentage you see in the stats boxes.

As you might imagine, pitchers with a higher CSP are more likely to work in the zone, where pitchers with a lower CSP are likely locating their pitches outside the normal strike zone, for better or for worse.

Projections

Many of you aren't turning to this book just for a look at what a player has done, but for a look at what a player is going to do: the PECOTA projections. PECOTA, initially developed by Nate Silver (who has moved on to greater fame as a political analyst), consists of three parts:

1. Major-league equivalencies, which use minor-league statistics to project how a player will perform in the major leagues;
2. Baseline forecasts, which use weighted averages and regression to the mean to estimate a player's current true talent level; and
3. Aging curves, which uses the career paths of comparable players to estimate how a player's statistics are likely to change over time.

With all those important things covered, let's take a look at what's in the book this year.

Team Prospectus

Most of this book is composed of team chapters, with one for each of the 30 major-league franchises. On the first page of each chapter, you'll see a box that contains some of the key statistics for each team as well as a very inviting stadium diagram. (You can see an example of this for the Milwaukee Brewers on this very page!)

We start with the team name, their unadjusted 2019 win-loss record, and their divisional ranking. Beneath that are a host of other team statistics. **Pythag** presents an adjusted 2019 winning percentage, calculated by taking runs scored per game (**RS/G**) and runs allowed per game (**RA/G**) for the team, and running them through a version of Bill James' Pythagorean formula that was refined and improved by David Smyth and Brandon Heipp. (The formula is called "Pythagenpat," which is equally fun to type and to say.)

Next up is **DRC+**, described earlier, to indicate the overall hitting ability of the team either above or below league-average. Run prevention on the pitching side is covered by **DRA** (also mentioned earlier) and another metric: Fielding Independent Pitching (**FIP**), which calculates another ERA-like statistic based on strikeouts, walks, and home runs recorded. Defensive Efficiency Rating (**DER**) tells us the percentage of balls in play turned into outs for the team, and is a quick fielding shorthand that rounds out run prevention.

After that, we have several measures related to roster composition, as opposed to on-field performance. **B-Age** and **P-Age** tell us the average age of a team's batters and pitchers, respectively. **Salary** is the combined team payroll for all on-field players, and Doug Pappas' Marginal Dollars per Marginal Win (**M$/MW**) tells us how much money a team spent to earn production above replacement level.

Ending this batch of statistics is the number of disabled list days a team had over the season (**IL Days**) and the amount of salary paid to players on the disabled list (**$ on IL**); this final number is expressed as a percentage of total payroll.

Next to each of these stats, we've listed each team's MLB rank in that category from first to 30th. In this, first always indicates a positive outcome and 30th a negative outcome, except in the case of salary—first is highest.

After the franchise statistics, we share a few items about the team's home ballpark. There's the aforementioned diagram of the park's dimensions (including distances to the outfield wall), a graphic showing the height of the wall from the left-field pole to the right-field pole, and a table showing three-year park factors for the stadium. The park factors are displayed as indexes where 100 is average, 110 means that the park inflates the statistic in question by 10 percent, and 90 means that the park deflates the statistic in question by 10 percent.

On the second page of each team chapter, you'll find three graphs. The first is the **2019 Hit List Ranking**. This shows our Hit List Rank for the team on each day of the 2019 season and is intended to give you a picture of the ups and downs of the team's season. Hit List Rank measures overall team performance and drives the Hit List Power Rankings at the baseballprospectus.com website.

The second graph is **Committed Payroll** and helps you see how the team's payroll has compared to the MLB and divisional average payrolls over time. Payroll figures are current as of January 1, 2020; with so many free agents still unsigned as of this writing, the final 2020 figure will likely be significantly different for many teams. (In the meantime, you can always find the most current data at Baseball Prospectus' Cot's Baseball Contracts page.)

The third graph is **Farm System Ranking** and displays how the Baseball Prospectus prospect team has ranked the organization's farm system since 2007.

After the graphs, we have a **Personnel** section that lists many of the important decision-makers and upper-level field and operations staff members for the franchise, as well as any former Baseball Prospectus staff members who are currently part of the organization. (In very rare circumstances, someone might be on both lists!)

www.baseballprospectus.com

Juan Soto LF
Born: 10/25/98 Age: 21 Bats: L Throws: L
Height: 6'1" Weight: 185 Origin: International Free Agent, 2015

YEAR	TEAM	LVL	AGE	PA	R	2B	3B	HR	RBI	BB	K	SB	CS	AVG/OBP/SLG
2017	NAT	RK	18	27	3	1	1	0	4	2	1	0	0	.320/.370/.440
2017	HAG	A	18	96	15	5	0	3	14	10	8	1	2	.360/.427/.523
2018	HAG	A	19	74	12	5	3	5	24	14	13	2	0	.373/.486/.814
2018	POT	A+	19	73	17	3	1	7	18	11	8	0	1	.371/.466/.790
2018	HAR	AA	19	35	4	2	0	2	10	4	7	1	0	.323/.400/.581
2018	WAS	MLB	19	494	77	25	1	22	70	79	99	5	2	.292/.406/.517
2019	WAS	MLB	20	659	110	32	5	34	110	108	132	12	1	.282/.401/.548
2020	WAS	MLB	21	630	92	30	3	35	102	85	123	5	2	.284/.382/.543

Comparables: Ronald Acuña Jr., Mike Trout, Tony Conigliaro

YEAR	TEAM	LVL	AGE	PA	DRC+	VORP	BABIP	BRR	FRAA	WARP
2017	NAT	RK	18	27	135	1.5	.333	0.0	RF(9): -1.1	0.0
2017	HAG	A	18	96	181	8.0	.373	1.0	RF(19): -1.9, LF(2): -0.3	0.9
2018	HAG	A	19	74	222	14.5	.405	0.3	RF(14): 1.1, CF(2): 0.2	1.2
2018	POT	A+	19	73	260	15.4	.340	1.4	RF(14): 1.0, LF(1): 0.0	1.6
2018	HAR	AA	19	35	113	3.6	.364	0.0	LF(4): 0.6, RF(4): -0.5	0.1
2018	WAS	MLB	19	494	125	40.5	.338	-0.5	LF(114): 2.7	3.0
2019	WAS	MLB	20	659	136	49.0	.312	1.4	LF(150): -0.8	4.9
2020	WAS	MLB	21	630	133	43.6	.310	-0.1	LF 3	4.8

Position Players

After all that information and a thoughtful bylined essay covering each team, we present our player comments. These are also bylined, but due to frequent franchise shifts during the offseason, our bylines are more a rough guide than a perfect accounting of who wrote what.

Each player is listed with the major-league team that employed him as of early January 2020. If a player changed teams after that point via free agency, trade, or any other method, you'll be able to find them in the chapter for their previous squad.

As an example, take a look at the player comment for Nationals outfielder Juan Soto: the stat block that accompanies his written comment is at the top of this page. First we cover biographical information (age is as of June 30, 2020) before moving onto the stats themselves. Our statistic columns include standard identifying information like **YEAR**, **TEAM**, **LVL** (level of affiliated play) and **AGE** before getting into the numbers. Next, we provide raw, untranslated numbers like you might find on the back of your dad's baseball cards: **PA** (plate appearances), **R** (runs), **2B** (doubles), **3B** (triples), **HR** (home runs), **RBI** (runs batted in), **BB** (walks), **K** (strikeouts), **SB** (stolen bases) and **CS** (caught stealing).

Statistical Introduction - xi

Next, we have unadjusted "slash" statistics: **AVG** (batting average), **OBP** (on-base percentage) and **SLG** (slugging percentage). Following the slash line is **DRC+** (Deserved Runs Created Plus), which we described earlier as total offensive expected contribution compared to the league average.

One of our oldest active metrics, **VORP** (Value Over Replacement Player), considers offensive production, position and plate appearances. In essence, it is the number of runs contributed beyond what a replacement-level player at the same position would contribute if given the same percentage of team plate appearances. VORP does not consider the quality of a player's defense.

BABIP (batting average on balls in play) tells us how often a ball in play fell for a hit, and can help us identify whether a batter may have been lucky or not...but note that high BABIPs also tend to follow the great hitters of our time, as well as speedy singles hitters who put the ball on the ground.

The next item is **BRR** (Baserunning Runs), which covers all of a player's baserunning accomplishments including (but not limited to) swiped bags and failed attempts. Next is **FRAA** (Fielding Runs Above Average), which also includes the number of games previously played at each position noted in parentheses. Multi-position players have only their two most frequent positions listed here, but their total FRAA number reflects all positions played.

Our last column here is **WARP** (Wins Above Replacement Player). WARP estimates the total value of a player, which means for hitters it takes into account hitting runs above average (calculated using the DRC+ model), BRR and FRAA. Then, it makes an adjustment for positions played and gives the player a credit for plate appearances based upon the difference between "replacement level"—which is derived from the quality of players added to a team's roster after the start of the season–and the league average.

The final line just below the stats box is **PECOTA** data, which is discussed further in a following section.

Catchers

Catchers are a special breed, and thus they have earned their own separate box which displays some of the defensive metrics that we've built just for them. As an example, let's check out J.T. Realmuto.

The **YEAR** and **TEAM** columns match what you'd find in the other stat box. **P. COUNT** indicates the number of pitches thrown while the catcher was behind the plate, including swinging strikes, fouls and balls in play. **FRM RUNS** is the total run value the catcher provided (or cost) his team by influencing the umpire to call strikes where other catchers did not. **BLK RUNS** expresses the total run value above or below average for the catcher's ability to prevent wild pitches and passed balls. **THRW RUNS** is calculated using a similar model as the previous two statistics, and it measures a catcher's ability to throw out basestealers but also to dissuade them from testing his arm in the first place. It takes into account factors like the pitcher (including his delivery and pickoff move) and baserunner (who could be as fast as Billy Hamilton or as slow as Yonder Alonso). **TOT RUNS** is the sum of all of the previous three statistics.

Justin Verlander   RHP
Born: 02/20/83   Age: 37   Bats: R   Throws: R
Height: 6'5"   Weight: 225   Origin: Round 1, 2004 Draft (#2 overall)

YEAR	TEAM	LVL	AGE	W	L	SV	G	GS	IP	H	HR	BB/9	K/9	K	GB%	BABIP
2017	DET	MLB	34	10	8	0	28	28	172	153	23	3.5	9.2	176	34%	.283
2017	HOU	MLB	34	5	0	0	5	5	34	17	4	1.3	11.4	43	32%	.194
2018	HOU	MLB	35	16	9	0	34	34	214	156	28	1.6	12.2	290	31%	.272
2019	HOU	MLB	36	21	6	0	34	34	223	137	36	1.7	12.1	300	36%	.219
2020	HOU	MLB	37	15	6	0	29	29	184	138	28	2.3	12.1	248	35%	.274

Comparables: Zack Greinke, A.J. Burnett, Aníbal Sánchez

YEAR	TEAM	LVL	AGE	WHIP	ERA	DRA	WARP	MPH	FB%	WHF	CSP
2017	DET	MLB	34	1.28	3.82	4.03	3.0	97.7	58	11	47.8
2017	HOU	MLB	34	0.65	1.06	3.08	0.9	97.5	59.6	15.1	49.9
2018	HOU	MLB	35	0.90	2.52	2.33	7.3	97.5	61.2	16.2	51.6
2019	HOU	MLB	36	0.80	2.58	2.51	7.9	96.8	49.9	17.5	48.3
2020	HOU	MLB	37	1.01	2.75	2.95	5.3	95.8	54.6	15.1	48.2

Pitchers

Let's give our pitchers a turn, using 2019 AL Cy Young winner Justin Verlander as our example. Take a look at his stat block: the first line and the **YEAR**, **TEAM**, **LVL** and **AGE** columns are the same as in the position player example earlier.

Here too, we have a series of columns that display raw, unadjusted statistics compiled by the pitcher over the course of a season: **W** (wins), **L** (losses), **SV** (saves), **G** (games pitched), **GS** (games started), **IP** (innings pitched), **H** (hits allowed) and **HR** (home runs allowed). Next we have two statistics that are rates: **BB/9** (walks per nine innings) and **K/9** (strikeouts per nine innings), before returning to the unadjusted K (strikeouts).

Next up is **GB%** (ground ball percentage), which is the percentage of all batted balls that were hit on the ground, including both outs and hits. Remember, this is based on observational data and subject to human error, so please approach this with a healthy dose of skepticism.

BABIP (batting average on balls in play) is calculated using the same methodology as it is for position players, but it often tells us more about a pitcher than it does a hitter. With pitchers, a high BABIP is often due to poor defense or bad luck, and can often be an indicator of potential rebound, and a low BABIP may be cause to expect performance regression. (A typical league-average BABIP is close to .290-.300.)

The metrics **WHIP** (walks plus hits per inning pitched) and **ERA** (earned run average) are old standbys: WHIP measures walks and hits allowed on a per-inning basis, while ERA measures earned runs on a nine-inning basis. Neither of these stats are translated or adjusted.

DRA (Deserved Run Average) was described at length earlier, and measures how many runs the pitcher "deserved" to allow per nine innings. Please note that since we lack all the data points that would make for a "real" DRA for minor-league events, the DRA displayed for minor league partial-seasons is based off of different data. (That data is a modified version of our cFIP metric, which you can find more information about on our website.)

Just like with hitters, **WARP** (Wins Above Replacement Player) is a total value metric that puts pitchers of all stripes on the same scale as position players. We use DRA as the primary input for our calculation of WARP. You might notice that relief pitchers (due to their limited innings) may have a lower WARP than you were expecting or than you might see in other WARP-like metrics. WARP does not take leverage into account, just the actions a pitcher performs and the expected value of those actions...which ends up judging high-leverage relief pitchers differently than you might imagine given their prestige and market value.

MPH gives you the pitcher's 95th percentile velocity for the noted season, in order to give you an idea of what the *peak* fastball velocity a pitcher possesses. Since this comes from our pitch-tracking data, it is not publicly available for minor-league pitchers.

Finally, we display the three new pitching metrics we described earlier. **FB%** (fastball percentage) gives you the percentage of fastballs thrown out of all pitches. **WHF** (whiff rate) tells you the percentage of swinging strikes induced out of all pitches. **CSP** (called strike probability) expresses the likelihood of all pitches thrown to result in a called strike, after controlling for factors like handedness, umpire, pitch type, count and location.

PECOTA

All players have PECOTA projections for 2020, as well as a set of other numbers that describe the performance of comparable players according to PECOTA. All projections for 2020 are for the player at the date we went to press in early January and are projected into the league and park context as indicated by the team abbreviation. (Note that players at very low levels of the minors are too unpredictable to assess using these numbers.) All PECOTA projected statistics represent a player's projected major-league performance.

Below the projections are the player's three highest-scoring comparable players as determined by PECOTA. All comparables represent a snapshot of how the listed player was performing at the same age as the current player, so if a

23-year-old pitcher is compared to Bartolo Colón, he's actually being compared to a 23-year-old Colón, not the version that pitched for the Rangers in 2018, nor to Colón's career as a whole.

A few points about pitcher projections. First, we aren't yet projecting peak velocity, so that column will be blank in the PECOTA lines. Second, projecting DRA is trickier than evaluating past performance, because it is unclear how deserving each pitcher will be of his anticipated outcomes. However, we know that another DRA-related statistic–contextual FIP or cFIP-estimates future run scoring very well. So for PECOTA, the projected DRA figures you see are based on the past cFIPs generated by the pitcher and comparable players over time, along with the other factors described above.

Lineouts

In each chapter's Lineouts section, you'll find abbreviated text comments, as well as all the same information you'd find in our full player comments. The only difference is that we limit the stats boxes in this section to only including the 2019 information for each player.

Managers

After all those wonderful team chapters, we've got statistics for each big-league manager, all of whom are organized by alphabetical order. Here you'll find a block including an extraordinary amount of information collected from each manager's entire career. For more information on the acronyms and what they mean, please visit the Glossary at www.baseballprospectus.com.

There is one important metric that we'd like to call attention to, and you'll find it next to each manager's name: **wRM+** (weighted reliever management plus). Developed by Rob Arthur and Rian Watt, wRM+ investigates how good a manager is at using their best relievers during the moments of highest leverage, using both our proprietary DRA metric as well as Leverage Index. wRM+ is scaled to a league average of 100, and a wRM+ of 105 indicates that relievers were used approximately five percent "better" than average. On the other hand, a wRM+ of 95 would tell us the team used its relievers five percent "worse" than the average team.

While wRM+ does not have an extremely strong correlation with a manager, it is statistically significant; this means that a manager is not *entirely* responsible for a team's wRM+, but does have some effect on that number.

PECOTA Leaderboards

If you're familiar with PECOTA, then you'll have noticed that the projection system often appears bullish on players coming off a bad year and bearish on players coming off a good year. (This is because the system weights several previous seasons, not just the most recent one.) In addition, we publish the 50th

Kansas City Royals 2020

percentile projections for each player–which is smack in the middle of the range of projected production—which tends to mean PECOTA stat lines don't often have extreme results like 40 home runs or 250 strikeouts in a given season. In essence, PECOTA doesn't project very many extreme seasons.

At the end of the book, we've ranked the top players at each position based on their PECOTA projections. This might help you visualize just how a given player's projection compares to that of their peers, so that even if a dramatic stat line isn't projected, you can still imagine how they stack up against the rest of the league. ∎

Part 1: Team Analysis

Kansas City Royals: Where Are You Going, Where Have You Been?

Lucas Apostoleris, Ben Spanier and Matthew Trueblood

2019: What Went Right

For a team that spent the entirety of the year at or near the bottom of the AL Central, there were a few bright spots worth noting. Whit Merrifield continued his solid production since becoming a regular in 2017 at the age of 28, slashing .303/.348/463, good for a 110 DRC+. Primarily a second baseman, Merrifield's versatility was also a plus: He spent time in all three outfield positions this year as well as at first base. Third baseman Hunter Dozier who, like Merrifield, is something of a late-bloomer at age 27, was also a positive in the infield. After a disappointing -1.5 WARP showing in 2018, Dozier got off to a blazing start, hitting .349/.447/.646 through the end of April. He cooled off from that pace, but his season DRC+ of 118 and WARP of 3.0 were still mighty fine. Like Merrifield, Dozier also saw time in the outfield this year, starting 17 games as the team's right fielder. This foreshadowed a possible full-time move to the pastures for 2020.

Dozier's challenger for Royals Breakout Player of the Year was DH/RF Jorge Soler, who the Royals acquired from the Cubs for closer Wade Davis prior to the 2017 season. Soler was a top prospect with Chicago and has been trying to establish himself as a regular since 2014, but 2019 was the first season where he truly leveraged his prodigious power skills: He was the first Royals player to reach 40 home runs and when Mike Trout stuck at 45 due to injury, Soler sailed past him to lead the league with 48.

Royals pitching was like a bad book where the best parts were the first page (Opening Day starter Brad Keller) and the last page (closer Ian Kennedy)—just don't ask about the rest. After being taken in the 2017 Rule 5 Draft, Keller turned in a nice surprise of a rookie season. After a rough first half (4.47 ERA) he made some adjustments and had a stronger second half (3.62 ERA) before being shut down at the end of August; all told, he pitched to a 102 DRA- and 1.4 WARP—roughly league-average performance for a pitcher with a lot of years ahead of him.

After being bumped from the starting rotation, the veteran Kennedy stepped in nicely as the team's closer for much of the season. Moving to a short-relief role led him to his highest strikeout rate (27.4 percent of batters faced) and fastball velocity (94.8 mph average four-seamer) in any season of his 13-year career. Kennedy finished with a 72 DRA-, his best mark since his 2014 season with the Padres (68). Joining him on the lonely positive side of the bullpen ledger was rookie righty Scott Barlow, who showed some promise as a setup man with impressive strikeout numbers and rebounded from a 6.19 ERA-first half to mark a 2.12 ERA in 34 post-break innings, albeit with a troubling 5.3 walks per nine innings.

2019: What Went Wrong

The Royals went 59-103, reaching 100 losses for the second year in a row. On the hitting side, a key injury and a trio of anemic performances from key players kept the Royals' offense from being even average. Shortstop Adalberto Mondesi seemed poised to build off his strong second-half in 2018. Slowed by injuries to his groin muscle and left shoulder which caused him to miss 60 games, he hit just .263/.291/.424—not exactly the step forward that the Royals were hoping for, though we can't forget that he just turned 24 in July.

First baseman Ryan O'Hearn came up for the last two months of the 2018 season and made a good first impression, slugging .597 with 12 home runs in his 44 games. There would be no encore: In 370 plate appearances surrounding a six-week demotion to Triple-A Omaha, O'Hearn hit just .195/.281/.369—breaking down to .188/.286/.333 before, .204/.274/.415 after. He'll get another shot in 2020.

Middle-infielder Nicky Lopez was another young player for whom the Royals had high hopes. The contact-oriented Lopez was hitting .353/.457/.500 with four times as many walks as strikeouts when he was called up from Omaha in mid-May, but his minor-league success did not translate to the big-league level: Lopez hit .240/.276/.325, and despite solid defense finished precisely at replacement level. Free-agent outfielder Billy Hamilton was signed to a one-year contract over the offseason, and while he had never been a menace at the plate, the Royals hoped they could get enough offensive value out of him that his always-excellent defense could supply the rest of a winning package. He played 93 games with the team, hitting .211/.275/.269 with no homers and saw his playing time begin to decline by the All-Star break. He was waived in mid-August before being claimed by the Braves.

The pitching staff had the fourth-worst ERA in the major leagues; beyond Keller and Kennedy there were few positives. Danny Duffy, at one point one of the stars of the team and rewarded with a five-year contract prior to the 2017 season, continued his decline with an injury-plagued year; it took a strong September to get his ERA down to 4.34. More than 250 innings were committed to swingmen Glenn Sparkman and Jorge López and they rewarded the team with a combined WARP of -5.5. —*Lucas Apostoleris*

Prospect Outlook

The Royals are bad. They had the second pick in the 2019 draft and will pick fourth in 2020, which represents not so much improvement as the presence of teams that were even worse. The change in ownership to John Sherman represents a potentially destabilizing change. That would be unfortunate timing as help is on the way and it's not too far off. Kansas City has four arms in the mid-to-upper minors with legitimate middle of the rotation potential and maybe more: **Brady Singer** and **Jackson Kowar** at Double-A Northwest Arkansas, and lefties **Daniel Lynch** and **Kris Bubic** at High-A Wilmington. If you asked four evaluators their favorite you might get four different answers.

So, what's not to like? Well, the hitters. Three would-be cornerstones of a future division contender began the year at Wilmington and ended it there, all finishing below the Mendoza line. Catcher **MJ Melendez** and first baseman **Nick Pratto** slogged through their age-20 seasons while powerful outfielder **Seuly Matias** scuffled for two months before injury befell him. Center fielder **Kyle Isbel** fared the best of the Carolina quartet, starting off scalding before (just their luck) missing two months due to injury and slumping upon his return. The Royals farm system is a land of contrasts. —*Ben Spanier*

2020 Outlook

Sherman's arrival hasn't caused immediate or massive ripples of change to the team's day-to-day operation, nor its core philosophy. Dayton Moore went ahead with the succession plan he'd plotted a year in advance, installing Mike Matheny as the successor to Ned Yost on the top step of the dugout. For a team that still does several things in a somewhat old-fashioned way (even while paying lip service to advanced information and evolving player-development practices), Matheny is a good fit, although that doesn't mean there weren't better managers out there. In his years with the Cardinals, Matheny never faced the challenge that is managing a team with low expectations. That changes starting when pitchers and catchers report to spring training, and it will be up to Matheny to prove he has more range than he'd previously shown.

Moore was less aggressive about adding potentially tradable veterans at the nadir of their value, mostly for good reasons: The Royals now have talented young players at whom they might want to get extended looks. Maikel Franco

Kansas City Royals 2020

was the big signing of the winter, but he's less a flippable asset than a potential change-of-scenery guy on whose power and pliability the team is willing to gamble a little. Alex Gordon also re-signed, all but ensuring he'll be a career Royal. That's the kind of no-brainer every organization should get right, but many teams miss such chances these days, so the Royals deserve kudos for working to make Gordon feel welcome and wanted, even as his decline continues and his prospects for everyday playing time dim. —*Matthew Trueblood*

Performance Graphs

2019 Hit List Ranking

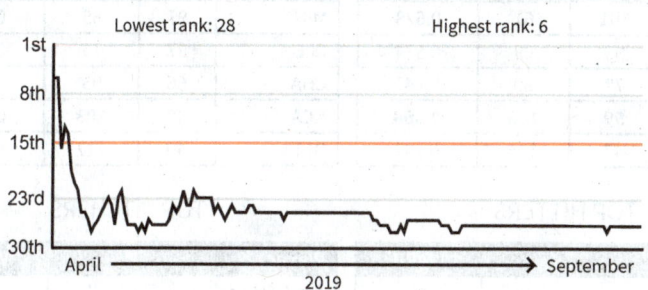

Committed Payroll (in millions)

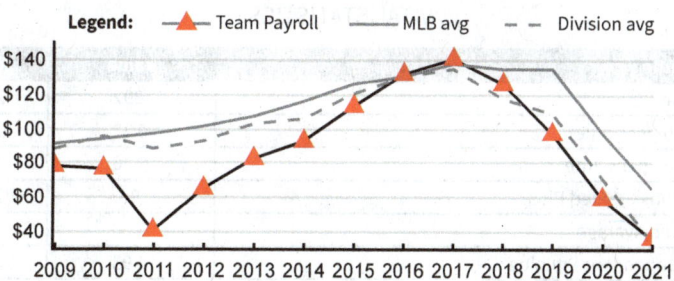

Farm System Ranking

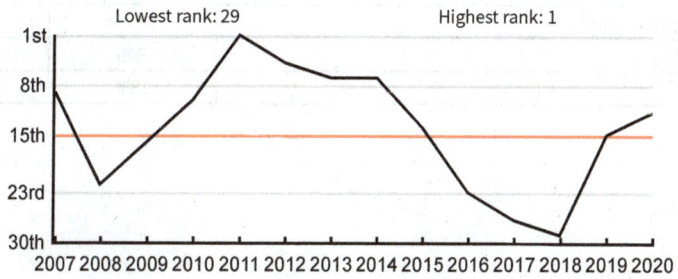

2019 Team Performance

ACTUAL STANDINGS

Team	W	L	Pct
MIN	101	61	0.623
CLE	93	69	0.574
CHA	72	89	0.447
KCA	**59**	**103**	**0.364**
DET	47	114	0.292

THIRD-ORDER STANDINGS

Team	W	L	Pct
MIN	97	65	0.597
CLE	87	75	0.535
CHA	66	95	0.412
KCA	**59**	**103**	**0.364**
DET	49	112	0.304

TOP HITTERS

Player	WARP
Jorge Soler	4.5
Hunter Dozier	3.0
Whit Merrifield	3.0

TOP PITCHERS

Player	WARP
Brad Keller	1.4
Ian Kennedy	1.3
Jake Diekman	1.2

VITAL STATISTICS

Statistic Name	Value	Rank
Pythagenpat	.392	27th
Runs Scored per Game	4.27	26th
Runs Allowed per Game	5.36	23rd
Deserved Runs Created Plus	90	23rd
Deserved Run Average	6.00	30th
Fielding Independent Pitching	4.93	26th
Defensive Efficiency Rating	.689	26th
Batter Age	27.6	10th
Pitcher Age	27.5	8th
Salary	$96.5M	24th
Marginal $ per Marginal Win	$8.0M	3rd
Injured List Days	809	4th
$ on IL	18%	20th

2020 Team Projections

PROJECTED STANDINGS

Team	W	L	Pct	+/-
MIN	93.4	68.6	0.577	-8
CLE	86.1	75.9	0.531	-7
CHA	82.5	79.5	0.509	10
DET	69.2	92.8	0.427	22
KCA	**67.8**	**94.2**	**0.419**	**9**

TOP PROJECTED HITTERS

Player	WARP
Jorge Soler	3.3
Whit Merrifield	2.8
Hunter Dozier	1.5

TOP PROJECTED PITCHERS

Player	WARP
Danny Duffy	0.8
Brad Keller	0.4
Jesse Hahn	0.3

FARM SYSTEM REPORT

Top Prospect	Number of Top 101 Prospects
Bobby Witt Jr., #29	4

KEY DEDUCTIONS

Player	WARP
Trevor Oaks	0.0

KEY ADDITIONS

Player	WARP
Maikel Franco	0.3
Greg Holland	0.1
Nick Heath	0.0
Stephen Woods Jr.	0.0
Brady Singer	0.0
Trevor Rosenthal	0.0
Matt Reynolds	-0.1
Foster Griffin	-0.1
Carlos Hernandez	-0.3
Jeison Guzman	-0.4

Team Personnel

Senior Vice President - Baseball Operations/General Manager
Dayton Moore

Assistant General Manager of Player Personnel
J.J. Picollo

Assistant General Manager of Major League and International Operations
Rene Francisco

Assistant General Manager
Scott Sharp

Manager
Mike Matheny

BP Alumni
Daniel Mack

Kauffman Stadium Stats

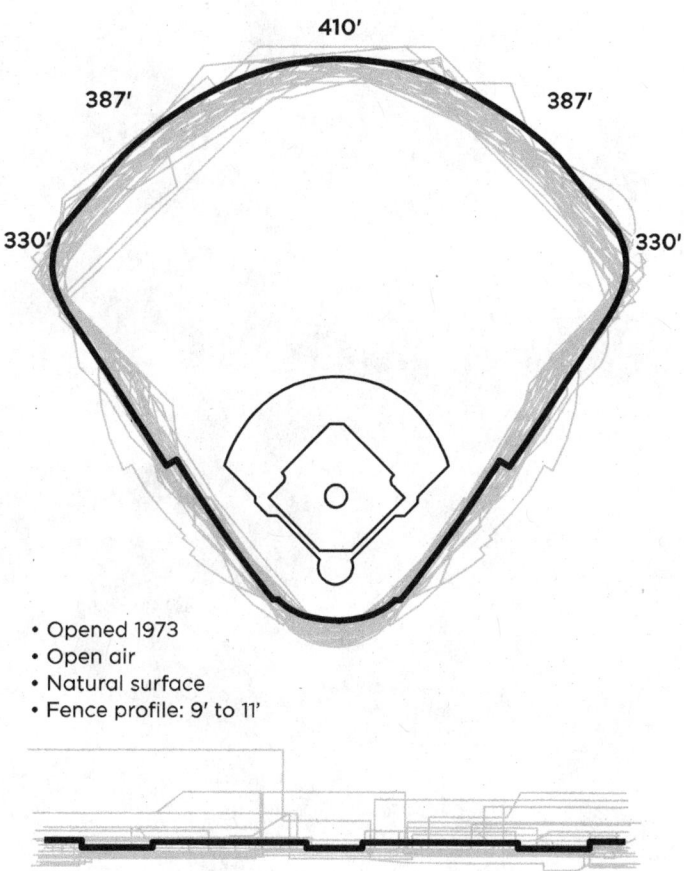

- Opened 1973
- Open air
- Natural surface
- Fence profile: 9' to 11'

Three-Year Park Factors

Runs	Runs/RH	Runs/LH	HR/RH	HR/LH
100	100	101	90	92

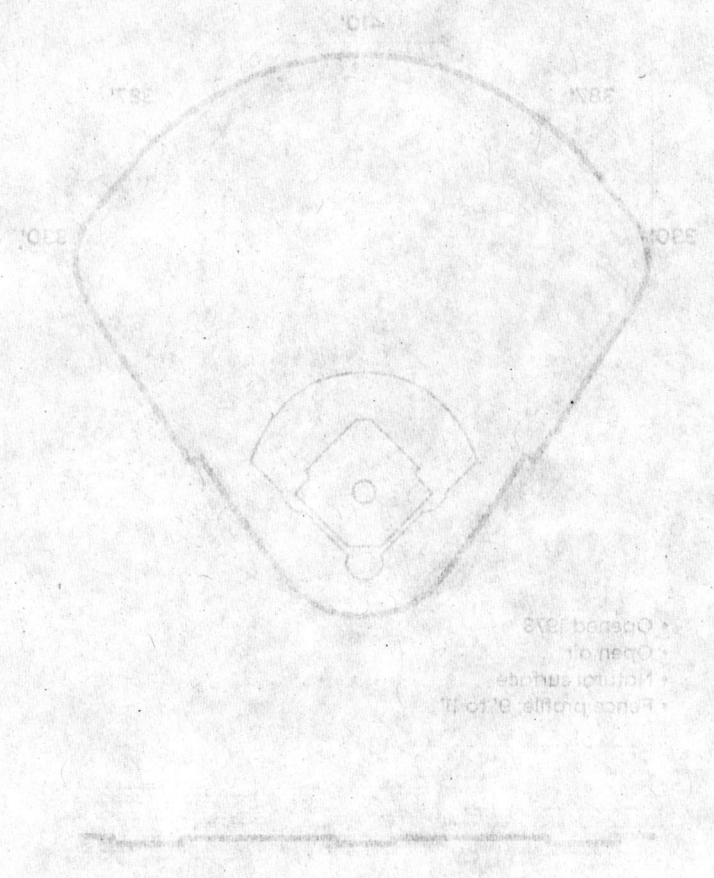

Royals Team Analysis

Over the last two decades, the Kansas City Royals have been a very unsuccessful team. During that time, the Royals have finished a season within seven games of first place in their division four times; they won it once, in 2015, which was also the year they won the World Series. Over that same period, they've finished more than 30 games out seven times and lost more than 100 games six times. Both tallies include the last two years and, at the risk of losing more results-oriented readers of this essay before the end of its fourth sentence, are likely to continue into the next one. The pitching is bad, the hitting is not what you could call "good" and the farm system is...well, it's hard to be as definitive here, but it's also unlikely to make much difference this season. They'll be bad in the same ways and for more or less the same reasons.

None of this is new, in short. The Royals are recursive in terms of their broader approach and their results, to the point where the organization appears to have lapped itself; as it happens, they already have another three-year stretch of 100 or more losses, between 2004 and 2006, on the ledger in recent memory. There are only so many ways a team can lose a game, but while the Royals tend to lock into grooves that last for whole presidential administrations at a time, the way in which they lose now is not the same way that they have always lost over the last 20 years. It's happening for the same fundamental reasons that it always has, which is that the organization is cheap and reactionary. But there are different ways for a team to be bad. Some of those ways of failing can be seen as pointing or building towards success. Some of them are just plain failure. The Royals have chosen, actively or passively, to lose during their decades of doing nothing but. The question is what they might someday get out of it.

Before tanking became a recognizable concept, let alone a process that could be spun as a tactical choice toward a competitive end, the Royals made it into something of an ethos. The futility of the worst Royals teams was visible in their records and some exceptionally rude stats—this is neither here nor there, but the 2005 and 2006 Royals were both 47 runs worse by run differential than any team in baseball—and in a deeper sense that was profound, unique, somehow almost spiritual. There was a deep and abiding purposelessness to those teams: a sense that they were rudderless, more or less by design.

The system intermittently delivered some rising stars, and they showed out without any apparent attempt being made to build around them; budgets were stable, but static. Some free agents came aboard every year into a career

Kansas City Royals 2020

hospice, and there enjoyed a quiet last turn or two around the league. Those odd stars the system produced squandered their early primes in Kansas City, generally with dignity and distinction, and then left in free agency without the team putting up much of a fight, or in deadline deals for the kind of interchangeable prospects the team developed on its own—corner infielders near the majors with plate discipline but no pop, or pop but no plate discipline and/or some live-armed, bullpen-bound pitchers named Mike or Luke. There was one flukey 83-win year in 2003, a false dawn that baseball historians may someday call the Randaissance, after the team's mainstay third baseman (although we should all hope they won't). Otherwise all that aimless futility went on for 13 years.

⚔ ⚔ ⚔

It wasn't just that the team didn't get better during that period (split roughly evenly between the GM tenures of Allard Baird and Dayton Moore), although they assuredly did not. It was that every move seemed to have been made with the intention of getting the team as close as possible to 95 losses without going over. Weird things happened in the purgatory that the team furnished for itself at the bottom of the American League Central. Ken Harvey made an All-Star team, then played just 12 more games in the bigs when that season was over. Ángel Berroa was Rookie of the Year, somehow. There was a lot of Bruce Chen on the monitors, just in general. A striking number of the names that filled out the rosters over that lost decade-and-a-half sound like characters from Charles Portis novels—Jimmy Gobble, Calvin Pickering, Tug Hulett, Everett Teaford, Runelvys Hernandez, Ross Gload.

It was never clear what Baird was trying to do during his years at the helm, but Moore, who was hired in 2006, is and was different. Moore has notched only three winning seasons in 13 years, but he has always given the impression that things were happening for a reason, even when that reason has been difficult to discern. "Let's just trust the process," Moore told the *Kansas City Star* in 2009. "If other people don't want to trust the process, that's fine. If other people want to abandon the process, then abandon it. I'm not abandoning the process. I believe in the process. You get a good group of people together. You work hard together. You trust in one another. You go through the difficult times. You work hard to make good decisions. You keep guys together and, eventually, it will happen."

Moore had overseen three awful seasons by that point and the Royals would lose 95, 91 and 90 games before they broke .500, but he also wasn't wrong. It really did happen, and then it ended. Moore got through the miserable years before and after because he made it seem as if there was some process to trust and because he made moves that, however well they fit with the relentless cheapness that was the team's core corporate value under previous ownership, did seem to be building toward some goal. He found value in the favorable draft positions that those miserable seasons afforded the team and also in later rounds—stealing Greg Holland in the 10th, Whit Merrifield in the ninth, Jarrod Dyson in the 50th—for a few years, and then went right back to missing as egregiously as Baird ever had.

When all those small wins prised open a competitive window in the middle of the decade, Moore pushed through it. He nailed every big move he made when the team made a push for 2015, some of which were quite risky. The championship team was sui generis, and a testament to both Moore's vision and ownership's patience and, when the time came, willingness to jump. They put exquisite and sadistic pressure on every team they played through their refusal to make mistakes, and every one of those teams eventually relented under that assault. All of this is true, which is to say that, albeit on the most generous timetable, Moore was right.

But it is also true that the team hasn't finished above .500 once in the four seasons since they won the dang World Series. It is true, too, that fans showed up in droves when the team was good, and continued to turn out in dwindling numbers as the on-field product faded toward mediocrity, but they stopped turning out once the gradual burial of the championship roster was complete. A million fewer people attended Royals games in 2019 than came to watch the 2016 club; the 2019 figure was nearly half as many as during the team's World Series run. This stands to reason, but all of it points back to the same question that Moore used to answer with "trust the process," and it amounts to what are you trying to do here. You may not be surprised to learn the answer.

"You ask if this year is different," Moore told MLB.com before the 2018 season. "It isn't. It really isn't. The purpose doesn't change. You hold true to the things you believe in and the things you've learned...If we play the game for the right reasons and we do it together, we'll compete. We'll win. That formula doesn't change." That team lost 104 games, and lost 103 the year after that. There is no reason to think that Moore's answer has changed. It is difficult to imagine what would change it.

⚾   ⚾   ⚾

The competitive justification for a team choosing to stink for years, on purpose, is complicated without being complex. It boils down to the fact that baseball is extremely hard, and that building a winning baseball team is difficult. It takes a long time to replenish a farm system, and even brilliant youngsters can bust for various reasons; bodies break and owners don't want to spend money even though they're making it hand over fist, and so on. There is no real parity in baseball beyond this stubborn and fundamental truth, but the difficulty of it all does level the playing field. It is inherent not just to the game but to the broader business and study of the game that everyone involved is going to fail often, and fail badly.

There are ways to deal with this, or at least try to mitigate it. Teams that can afford to do so take the same approach that venture capitalists do: spraying a bunch of money at an impossible problem in the understanding that most of the bets will necessarily be losers, but that the ones that hit (or even push) might be instructive going forward. In point of fact, "teams that can afford to do so" includes basically every MLB team; the Royals were owned by the billionaire Walmart scion David Glass until the very end of 2019, at which point they were sold, for a clean $1 billion, to Kansas City businessman John Sherman.

That approach works, generally, but because it's expensive and because it's considered gauche to pay retail in baseball owner circles, most teams prefer the model of minimizing costs where it's expensive—or, "the players who actually play the games"—and spending that money to figure out ways to get more for less, or more from less. What this means, for our purposes as people who care about baseball, is that owners are trying to figure out the least they can spend and still make money at the volume and rate to which they've become accustomed. There are all kinds of ways to make this seem more complex than it is, and various obfuscatory bits of jargon pass into and out of vogue, but all those faddish terms and tortured justifications obscure the same fact, which is that some teams don't try very hard to win the World Series.

Some owners do want to win a World Series, for the natural and healthy reasons that everyone that cares about baseball would like to win a World Series, which is that it's an extremely cool and very difficult thing to do. Many of them don't want it all that much, or anyway don't want it enough to jeopardize the profitability built into owning a franchise by spending money on players that could otherwise just not be spent at all. In the crudest bottom-line sense, it can be difficult to tell the difference between a rebuilding team—one that's swapping expensive veteran assets for cheaper and more volatile ones and letting green rookies flounder in games that count in the standings because they believe it will help them flourish under similar circumstances in due time—and one that is just losing games because it doesn't know what it's about, or because its priors and principles are off, or because it isn't really trying that hard to do anything in particular beyond kick the can down the road. Not every losing team is rebuilding. Some of them are just like that.

This is where The Dayton Moore Experience and the broader Royals gambit becomes difficult to assess. Moore knows what he knows and believes what he believes, and he has gotten some important things right. But, whether because of how little ownership gave him or how little ownership asked of him, he has also been allowed to go on failing righteously—in the same ways, and for the same reasons—for far longer than would seem justified or even justifiable. It might not have been Moore's preference to draft the more-signable Luke Hochevar over Clayton Kershaw and Max Scherzer and literally every other player drafted in 2006, but he did it all the same; Hochevar has his World Series ring, but he is out of baseball and Kershaw and Scherzer are...not, let's just say. Drafting and player development are hard, but when Moore stopped hitting on important picks—when he took Aaron Crow 13 picks before Mike Trout in 2009; or Christian Colón instead of Chris Sale and Yasmani Grandal in 2010; or Bubba Starling ahead of Anthony Rendon, Francisco Lindor, Javy Báez and George Springer a year later—he put more pressure on his belief in what it means to build and be a baseball team. It's difficult to trust a process when it stops delivering desirable outcomes.

Theoretically, anyway. Colón delivered the decisive hit in that 2015 World Series and hasn't done much else, but he has a co-starring role in millions of happy memories. Starling, who finally made it to the bigs in 2019 after remaking everything that once made him a prodigy, doesn't look like someone likely to have a long career, but he's having one now. Kyle Zimmer, whom the team made the fifth pick of the 2012 draft, clawed his way to the majors in 2019 at age 27; he was hit hard, but he saw his dream through. They are not the future of the Royals, and look unlikely to be integral parts of the next good Royals team, whenever that might arrive. They are proof of Moore's belief that people who play the game for the right reasons and value their opportunity and never quit can indeed make it, but they are also, relative to their peers, compelling proof that a more capacious or forward-thinking organizational approach might yield better on-field results. All the values that Moore has centered as part of his perpetual process are laudable enough, but they're not enough on their own to get the Royals anywhere in particular. If the goal is simply to Do The Right Things per a certain definition, then the Royals are indeed doing just fine. If the goal is something more pedestrian and concrete like Improve Baseball Outcomes In The Near Term, they are not. Once again, it's far from clear what the Royals are doing, or trying to do.

And yet there's no reason to think they're going to stop doing it. Faith and patience and fellowship are important, and, while those are also words politicians tend to use to conceal various craven cynicisms, there's no reason to think Moore is insincere in his belief. Getting a good group of people together and working hard together and trusting each other and all the rest is not a bad idea when it comes to building a baseball team, or a shed or anything else, but it is also not sufficient on its own. At some point, if this shed is ever going to get built, some of the good and faithful men called to the task are going to have to show up with tools.

—*David Roth is a former editor at Deadspin.*

Part 2: Player Analysis

PLAYER COMMENTS WITH GRAPHS

Humberto Arteaga SS
Born: 01/23/94 Age: 26 Bats: R Throws: R
Height: 6'1" Weight: 160 Origin: International Free Agent, 2010

YEAR	TEAM	LVL	AGE	PA	R	2B	3B	HR	RBI	BB	K	SB	CS	AVG/OBP/SLG
2017	NWA	AA	23	490	47	12	3	1	35	25	65	4	4	.258/.300/.305
2018	OMA	AAA	24	445	42	19	1	6	49	21	73	2	3	.292/.322/.386
2019	OMA	AAA	25	302	39	10	1	5	26	12	34	11	5	.299/.333/.394
2019	KCA	MLB	25	135	11	4	0	0	4	8	28	1	1	.197/.258/.230
2020	KCA	MLB	26	251	19	12	1	2	21	10	51	3	2	.242/.278/.326

Comparables: Tom Upton, Harold Castro, Yadiel Rivera

Arteaga repeated every level of the minor leagues and still managed to reach the majors at 25, which is kind of impressive in its own right. To be fair, his promotion could be described as a result of suction: Whit Merrifield's move to right forced Nicky Lopez to second, and when Adelberto Mondesi got hurt and Chris Owings imploded, Arteaga got sucked into the wake of the collective misery. It shouldn't happen again; the Venezuelan shortstop simply cannot hit, and also cannot stop himself from trying to hit. Instead, his major league career will serve as an example of the New Order of roster management, when teams start rebuilding before they have the necessary materials, and are forced to assemble baseball games out of spackle, tarp, and Humberto Arteagas.

YEAR	TEAM	LVL	AGE	PA	DRC+	VORP	BABIP	BRR	FRAA	WARP
2017	NWA	AA	23	490	61	0.3	.297	-3.1	SS(96): 2.6, 2B(19): -1.9	-0.1
2018	OMA	AAA	24	445	84	9.8	.337	-0.6	3B(51): -1.7, SS(31): -2.4	0.4
2019	OMA	AAA	25	302	79	1.4	.325	-3.7	SS(26): 4.8, 2B(22): 1.7	0.9
2019	KCA	MLB	25	135	68	0.9	.255	0.4	SS(36): -2.4, 2B(2): -0.1	-0.1
2020	KCA	MLB	26	251	58	-5.9	.299	-0.3	SS 0, 3B 0	-0.5

Humberto Arteaga, continued

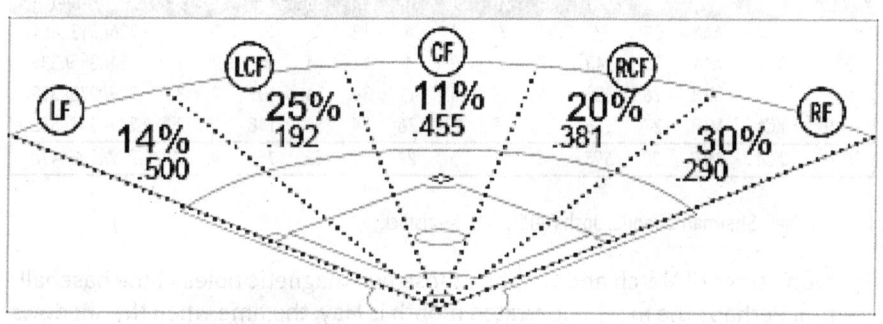

Batted Ball Distribution

Strike Zone vs LHP   *Strike Zone vs RHP*

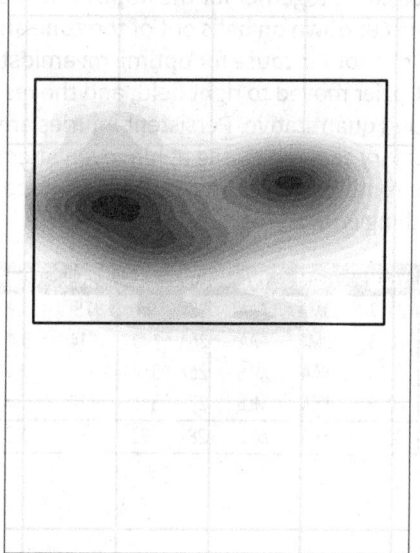

Hunter Dozier 3B/OF

Born: 08/22/91   Age: 28   Bats: R   Throws: R
Height: 6'4"   Weight: 220   Origin: Round 1, 2013 Draft (#8 overall)

YEAR	TEAM	LVL	AGE	PA	R	2B	3B	HR	RBI	BB	K	SB	CS	AVG/OBP/SLG
2017	OMA	AAA	25	96	11	6	1	4	12	9	37	1	1	.226/.313/.464
2018	OMA	AAA	26	143	18	7	0	1	11	24	43	2	1	.254/.385/.339
2018	KCA	MLB	26	388	36	19	4	11	34	24	109	2	3	.229/.278/.395
2019	KCA	MLB	27	586	75	29	10	26	84	55	148	2	2	.279/.348/.522
2020	KCA	MLB	28	595	65	25	5	21	73	52	164	4	2	.237/.308/.418

Comparables: Sherman Obando, Josh Fields, Jake Marisnick

Everyone sings of March and October, those two magnetic poles of the baseball season. Perhaps the most underrated month is May, the time when the shadows recede from the field, the games grow comfortable, and the clatter and bombast of April dies down. In May we have a moment to breathe, and to ask ourselves: *Is it real?* In Dozier's case, the answer was an emphatic yes. After a lengthy delay, it all came together for the hope of the post-championship youth movement, as he cut down on balls out of the zone and put more of his batted balls in the air. Yet another cause for optimism: amidst the team's post-deadline shakeup, Dozier moved to right field, and the results passed all the tests, both qualitative and quantitative. Persistent injuries are the biggest concern, as a June chest injury seemed to nag at him even after he returned to the lineup, but he finished strong. Having conquered spring, hopefully he'll get to find out what this fall thing is all about.

YEAR	TEAM	LVL	AGE	PA	DRC+	VORP	BABIP	BRR	FRAA	WARP
2017	OMA	AAA	25	96	75	3.9	.341	-0.3	RF(10): -0.1, 3B(7): -0.3	-0.2
2018	OMA	AAA	26	143	114	5.4	.392	-0.2	3B(19): 0.6, RF(13): 1.2	0.8
2018	KCA	MLB	26	388	80	-4.9	.296	-0.3	1B(51): -7.5, 3B(37): -5.9	-1.5
2019	KCA	MLB	27	586	118	33.4	.339	-1.8	3B(100): -0.3, RF(20): 0.4	3.0
2020	KCA	MLB	28	595	92	6.2	.301	-0.4	RF 4, 3B -1	1.0

Hunter Dozier, continued

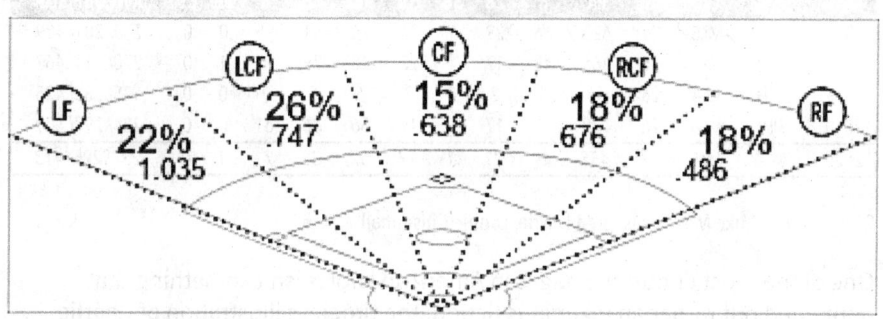

Batted Ball Distribution

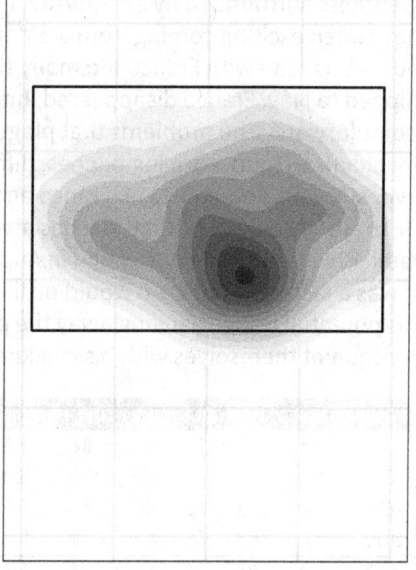

Maikel Franco 3B
Born: 08/26/92 Age: 27 Bats: R Throws: R
Height: 6'1" Weight: 215 Origin: International Free Agent, 2010

YEAR	TEAM	LVL	AGE	PA	R	2B	3B	HR	RBI	BB	K	SB	CS	AVG/OBP/SLG
2017	PHI	MLB	24	623	66	29	1	24	76	41	95	0	0	.230/.281/.409
2018	PHI	MLB	25	465	48	17	1	22	68	29	62	1	0	.270/.314/.467
2019	LEH	AAA	26	46	5	2	1	2	6	5	7	0	0	.175/.283/.425
2019	PHI	MLB	26	428	48	17	0	17	56	36	61	0	0	.234/.297/.409
2020	KCA	MLB	27	455	49	21	1	17	57	33	71	1	0	.237/.295/.413

Comparables: Mike Moustakas, Brett Lawrie, Lonnie Chisenhall

One of the most enduring images in American sports isn't something that happened but rather an ingenious fiction: the timeless illustration of Charlie Brown trying and failing to kick a football as Lucy Van Pelt yanks it away at the last second. Franco's four-and-a-half-year tenure with the Phillies had its moments was mostly been an exercise in briefly resplendent flashes of greatness surrounded by extreme disappointment. A seven-homer April would have been exciting coming from a different player, but Phillies fans had been down this road with Franco too many times. Sure enough, when the calendar flipped to May, Franco disappeared, hitting a woeful .227/.281/.374 from that point forward. The problems that plagued Franco in 2019—a long swing, poor mechanics, trouble driving pitches, difficulty elevating balls—have been present ever since his debut in 2014. Franco and the Phillies both diligently attempted to fix these issues, but hitting coaches aren't magicians and some flaws are just fatal. Philadelphia demoted him in August and while he returned in September, it was a taste of what 2020 would be like: Franco tantalizing a new fan base with his potential before yanking away the proverbial pigskin once pitchers reacquaint themselves with his weaknesses.

YEAR	TEAM	LVL	AGE	PA	DRC+	VORP	BABIP	BRR	FRAA	WARP
2017	PHI	MLB	24	623	82	1.2	.234	-1.8	3B(144): -9.2, 1B(2): -0.1	-0.3
2018	PHI	MLB	25	465	109	22.1	.270	1.5	3B(117): -2.7	2.1
2019	LEH	AAA	26	46	84	-0.5	.161	-0.3	3B(11): 0.9	0.1
2019	PHI	MLB	26	428	88	9.9	.236	-1.0	3B(110): 2.5, 1B(2): 0.0	1.1
2020	KCA	MLB	27	455	87	2.3	.248	-0.4	3B -2	0.0

Maikel Franco, continued

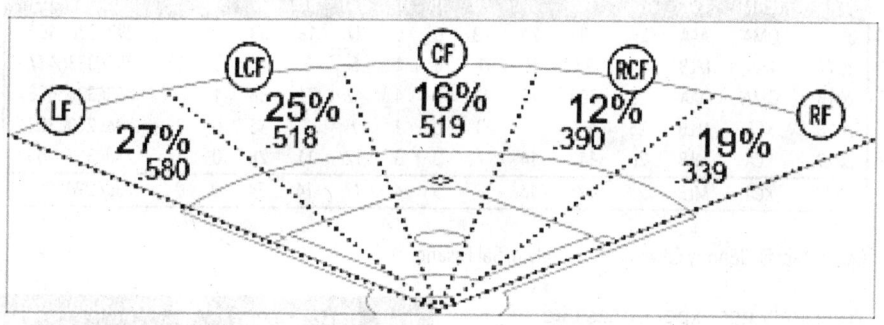

Batted Ball Distribution

| | Strike Zone vs LHP | Strike Zone vs RHP |

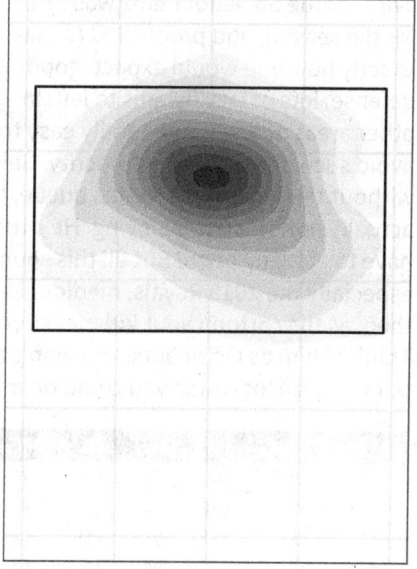

Royals Player Analysis - 25

Kansas City Royals 2020

Cam Gallagher   C

Born: 12/06/92   Age: 27   Bats: R   Throws: R
Height: 6'3"   Weight: 230   Origin: Round 2, 2011 Draft (#65 overall)

YEAR	TEAM	LVL	AGE	PA	R	2B	3B	HR	RBI	BB	K	SB	CS	AVG/OBP/SLG
2017	OMA	AAA	24	282	26	13	0	5	37	18	33	0	1	.292/.336/.400
2017	KCA	MLB	24	27	2	1	0	1	5	3	4	0	0	.250/.333/.417
2018	OMA	AAA	25	303	28	13	0	4	42	26	38	1	0	.265/.334/.358
2018	KCA	MLB	25	69	5	3	0	1	7	3	15	0	0	.206/.250/.302
2019	KCA	MLB	26	142	14	7	0	3	12	11	28	0	1	.238/.312/.365
2020	KCA	MLB	27	175	16	8	0	4	17	14	34	0	0	.230/.296/.352

Comparables: Johnny Edwards, Bob Melvin, Sal Fasano

You rarely get experiences like Gallagher outside of sports. The longtime backup stumbled into playing time when franchise icon/living statue Salvador Perez was lost for the season, and proceeded to play exactly how you would expect: good defense, lots of lazy flyballs to left. In other areas of life, it's generally easy to avoid such predictable mediocrity. Gallagher is the movie you scroll past without thinking in the Netflix queue, the music at the supermarket you don't actually notice is even playing. He's the can of cream of mushroom you never have to actually open. But all this sounds too negative; in the world, and especially the 2019 Royals, mediocrity can be a blessing. Think of Gallagher, then, as the cartoon your kid makes you watch that doesn't make you cringe. Think of him as Octonauts. You won't think about it when your kids get older, but there's a lot worse you could do in the world than Octonauts.

YEAR	TEAM	P. COUNT	FRM RUNS	BLK RUNS	THRW RUNS	TOT RUNS
2017	KCA	1026	-0.2	0.2	-0.1	0.6
2017	OMA	9981	11.1	1.6	1.0	14.1
2018	KCA	2387	1.5	1.0	0.0	2.6
2018	OMA	9812	11.3	0.3	0.1	11.4
2019	KCA	5498	3.7	0.9	-0.3	4.3
2020	KCA	6619	2.2	1.1	-0.4	2.9

YEAR	TEAM	LVL	AGE	PA	DRC+	VORP	BABIP	BRR	FRAA	WARP
2017	OMA	AAA	24	282	94	5.1	.317	-4.1	C(71): 11.8	2.0
2017	KCA	MLB	24	27	93	0.4	.263	-0.4	C(13): -0.2	0.0
2018	OMA	AAA	25	303	86	11.3	.294	-2.0	C(72): 11.9	2.0
2018	KCA	MLB	25	69	84	-1.9	.250	-1.6	C(20): 2.4	0.3
2019	KCA	MLB	26	142	92	6.0	.281	-0.6	C(44): 3.8	0.9
2020	KCA	MLB	27	175	71	1.0	.270	-0.7	C 2	0.3

Cam Gallagher, continued

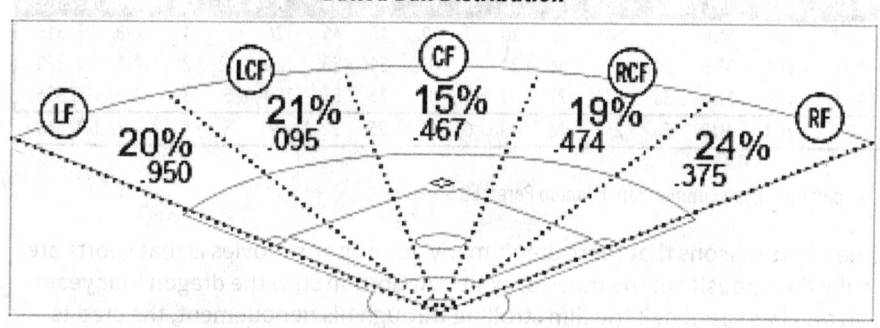
Batted Ball Distribution

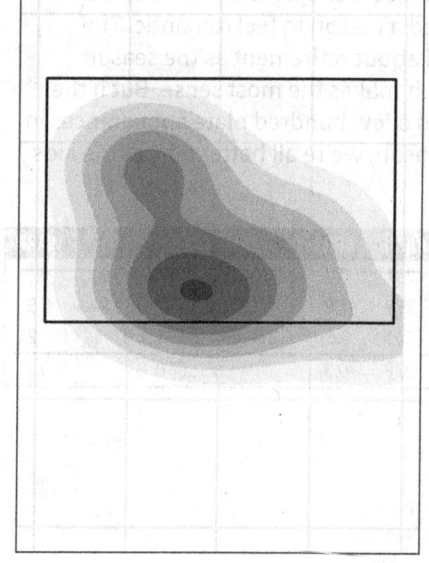
Strike Zone vs LHP

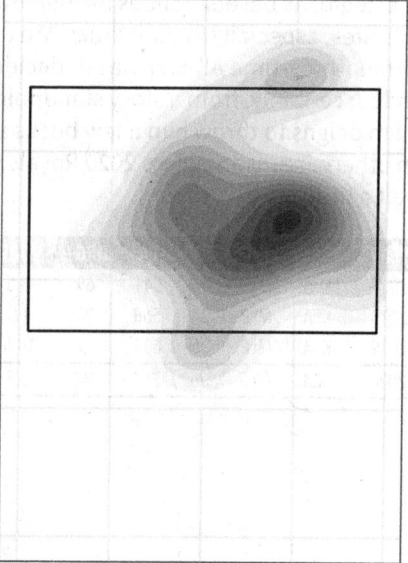
Strike Zone vs RHP

Kansas City Royals 2020

Alex Gordon LF

Born: 02/10/84 Age: 36 Bats: L Throws: R
Height: 6'1" Weight: 225 Origin: Round 1, 2005 Draft (#2 overall)

YEAR	TEAM	LVL	AGE	PA	R	2B	3B	HR	RBI	BB	K	SB	CS	AVG/OBP/SLG
2017	KCA	MLB	33	541	52	20	2	9	45	45	126	7	4	.208/.293/.315
2018	KCA	MLB	34	568	56	24	0	13	54	50	124	12	2	.245/.324/.370
2019	KCA	MLB	35	633	77	31	1	13	76	51	100	5	3	.266/.345/.396
2020	KCA	MLB	36	251	26	10	0	6	25	22	49	3	1	.235/.321/.360

Comparables: Ryan Zimmerman, Eduardo Perez, Ed Sprague

One of the reasons that there aren't many good sports movies is that sports are really the opposite of the movies. Exhibit A: Gordon slew the dragon four years ago and has spent half the film strolling through his denouement, the credits crawling up the screen. Also unlike the movies, it works just fine; narrative structure, it turns out, is overrated. Though the glory years recede into the distance, Gordon serves not only as a mentor, but as an absolutely vital source of esteem. As baseball slides further into asset management, we need fan favorites, especially in dark times. We need a reason to feel romantic. The former three-time All-Star was undecided about retirement as the season ended; certainly, from a story standpoint, it makes the most sense. But if the team deigns to throw him a few bucks and a few hundred plate appearances in an otherwise meaningless 2020 Royals season, we're all better off. Let the kids wait a little bit.

YEAR	TEAM	LVL	AGE	PA	DRC+	VORP	BABIP	BRR	FRAA	WARP
2017	KCA	MLB	33	541	69	-8.5	.261	-0.2	LF(140): 2.7, CF(15): -0.9	-0.5
2018	KCA	MLB	34	568	90	4.0	.299	-1.9	LF(125): 3.3, CF(11): -0.9	0.8
2019	KCA	MLB	35	633	97	14.8	.301	0.6	LF(146): -2.7, P(2): 0.0	1.2
2020	KCA	MLB	36	251	84	2.5	.279	-0.3	LF 0, CF 0	0.3

Alex Gordon, continued

Batted Ball Distribution

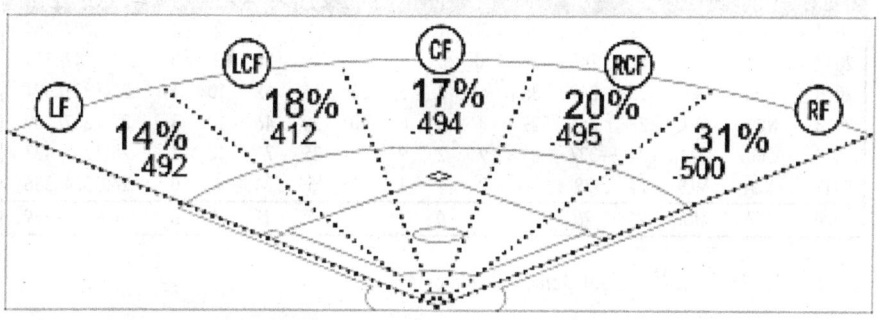

Strike Zone vs LHP   **Strike Zone vs RHP**

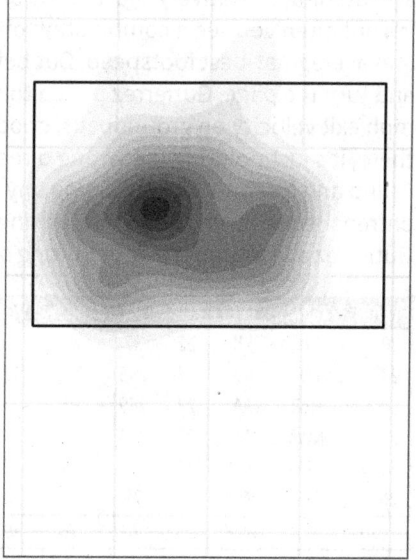

Kelvin Gutierrez   3B

Born: 08/28/94   Age: 25   Bats: R   Throws: R
Height: 6'3"   Weight: 215   Origin: International Free Agent, 2013

YEAR	TEAM	LVL	AGE	PA	R	2B	3B	HR	RBI	BB	K	SB	CS	AVG/OBP/SLG
2017	NAT	RK	22	37	6	3	1	0	1	4	7	2	0	.212/.297/.364
2017	POT	A+	22	245	34	10	6	2	16	19	59	3	0	.288/.347/.414
2018	HAR	AA	23	249	36	6	3	5	26	16	62	10	1	.274/.321/.391
2018	NWA	AA	23	264	29	8	3	6	40	20	46	10	3	.277/.337/.409
2019	OMA	AAA	24	327	41	9	2	9	43	35	71	12	1	.287/.367/.427
2019	KCA	MLB	24	79	4	2	1	1	11	5	24	1	0	.260/.304/.356
2020	KCA	MLB	25	70	6	3	0	1	7	5	19	1	0	.249/.306/.359

Comparables: Erik González, Brent Morel, Zoilo Almonte

It's not easy to imagine a player on the low end of a middling prospect list on a bad team and think "investment opportunity," but Gutierrez may just qualify. He offers a very rare combination of strengths and weaknesses: solid defense and arm at third, a relatively short swing and all the power of a Richard Marx album. It's not often you see a combination of that BABIP, a 68 percent groundball rate and average-at-best footspeed. But before you shout "regression," take a shot, and turn the page, Gutierrez pulled this trick off with not just luck but a 90.2 mph exit velocity on groundballs, good for 30th in baseball. The bat speed is there, it's just pointing the wrong direction. A broken toe thwarted a September callup and a chance at confirming any progress, and with Hunter Dozier entrenched at third, some enterprising, confident team might consider Gutierrez a fixer-upper worth putting some elbow grease into.

YEAR	TEAM	LVL	AGE	PA	DRC+	VORP	BABIP	BRR	FRAA	WARP
2017	NAT	RK	22	37	65	0.5	.269	0.8	3B(8): -1.1	0.0
2017	POT	A+	22	245	121	12.5	.380	2.0	3B(57): 6.4	2.2
2018	HAR	AA	23	249	96	9.3	.352	1.0	3B(56): 12.7, SS(1): 0.1	2.2
2018	NWA	AA	23	264	103	9.8	.321	1.3	3B(62): -0.7, SS(2): -0.2	1.0
2019	OMA	AAA	24	327	97	13.9	.349	2.3	3B(62): -3.3, 1B(7): -0.7	0.8
2019	KCA	MLB	24	79	67	-0.4	.367	-0.8	3B(18): -0.1	-0.1
2020	KCA	MLB	25	70	76	-0.6	.340	0.1	3B 0, 1B -1	-0.1

Kelvin Gutierrez, continued

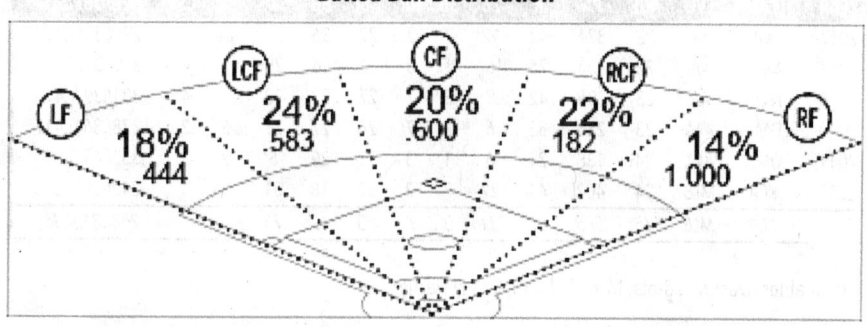

Strike Zone vs LHP   **Strike Zone vs RHP**

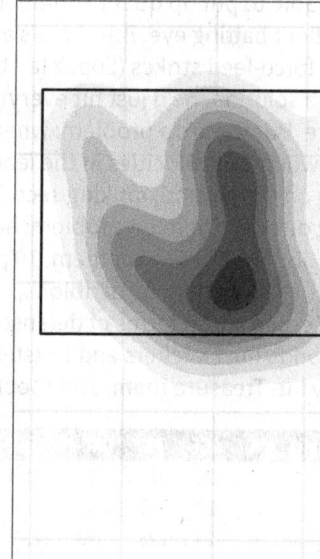

Nicky Lopez   MI

Born: 03/13/95   Age: 25   Bats: L   Throws: R
Height: 5'11"   Weight: 175   Origin: Round 5, 2016 Draft (#163 overall)

YEAR	TEAM	LVL	AGE	PA	R	2B	3B	HR	RBI	BB	K	SB	CS	AVG/OBP/SLG
2017	WIL	A+	22	324	42	12	7	2	27	36	23	14	8	.295/.376/.407
2017	NWA	AA	22	253	26	6	1	0	11	16	29	7	4	.259/.312/.293
2018	NWA	AA	23	325	42	8	5	2	27	33	23	9	4	.331/.397/.416
2018	OMA	AAA	23	256	33	6	2	7	26	27	29	6	2	.278/.364/.417
2019	OMA	AAA	24	138	27	6	1	3	13	20	5	9	3	.353/.457/.500
2019	KCA	MLB	24	402	44	22	2	2	30	18	51	1	1	.240/.276/.325
2020	KCA	MLB	25	595	53	31	3	6	53	42	75	12	5	.258/.316/.360

Comparables: Dustin Pedroia, Mike Richardt, Lenny Harris

Fans love prospects like Lopez, but in 2019 he proved, in the best and worst possible ways, why the David Fletcher role is such a difficult act to pull off. It's not about being good at one thing; you have to be good at so many things. Lopez was able to put up quality numbers in the minors in no small part thanks to his excellent batting eye. But there's a problem: major league pitchers knew they could force-feed strikes (Lopez led the league in pitches seen in the zone). Lopez had a solution: he'd just hit everything in the zone, ranking eighth in contact rate. But there's a problem: when he did put the bat on the ball, he had one of the worst exit velocities in the league. Lopez had a solution: he put everything on the ground, ranking second in baseball, and tried to run everything out. But there's a problem: he just wasn't fast enough to beat those grounders out, hitting .246 on them, 10 points above the league average. There's just always another roadblock, and while there's plenty of reason for optimism (especially in terms of defense), it just goes to show you what rare little diamonds the Fletchers and Ecksteins are: the league-average hitters who can't really hit. Treasure them, and root for Lopez to join them.

YEAR	TEAM	LVL	AGE	PA	DRC+	VORP	BABIP	BRR	FRAA	WARP
2017	WIL	A+	22	324	127	25.3	.315	0.8	SS(66): 4.4	2.8
2017	NWA	AA	22	253	70	5.2	.296	2.2	SS(33): -2.9, 2B(25): 2.5	0.4
2018	NWA	AA	23	325	123	25.9	.351	2.8	SS(58): -4.8, 2B(14): 0.4	1.9
2018	OMA	AAA	23	256	119	19.5	.294	0.0	SS(36): -1.0, 2B(18): 1.7	1.7
2019	OMA	AAA	24	138	140	15.1	.352	-1.3	SS(17): 3.5, 2B(14): 1.0	1.5
2019	KCA	MLB	24	402	61	-5.4	.273	2.5	2B(76): 1.3, SS(33): 1.2	0.0
2020	KCA	MLB	25	595	75	6.5	.290	2.1	2B 7, SS 0	1.4

Nicky Lopez, continued

Batted Ball Distribution

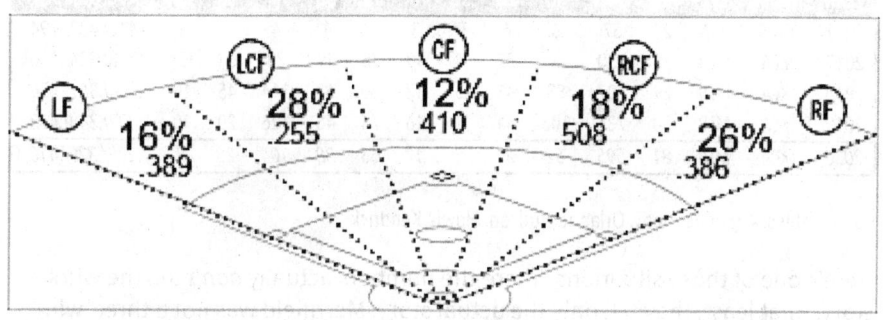

Strike Zone vs LHP   **Strike Zone vs RHP**

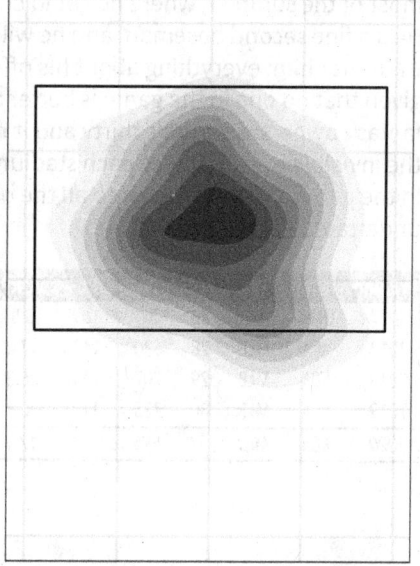

Whit Merrifield 2B

Born: 01/24/89 Age: 31 Bats: R Throws: R
Height: 6'0" Weight: 195 Origin: Round 9, 2010 Draft (#269 overall)

YEAR	TEAM	LVL	AGE	PA	R	2B	3B	HR	RBI	BB	K	SB	CS	AVG/OBP/SLG
2017	OMA	AAA	28	37	6	4	0	3	9	1	4	1	1	.412/.432/.794
2017	KCA	MLB	28	630	80	32	6	19	78	29	88	34	8	.288/.324/.460
2018	KCA	MLB	29	707	88	43	3	12	60	61	114	45	10	.304/.367/.438
2019	KCA	MLB	30	735	105	41	10	16	74	45	126	20	10	.302/.348/.463
2020	KCA	MLB	31	595	62	31	5	12	63	38	104	28	8	.279/.329/.418

Comparables: Adam Kennedy, Orlando Hudson, Howie Kendrick

Here's one of those situations where the numbers actually *don't* tell the whole story, or at least, they tell only the actual story. Merrifield was not a three-win player last year, despite the fact that he produced three wins in value; he was a four-win player forced to play like a three-win player. Stocked with young infield talent and cursed with Jorge Soler in right, the Royals moved Whit out there for most of the summer, where he could charitably be described as doing his best. He's a fine second baseman, and he will be again next year for whichever team trades for him; everything about his offense is as consistent as it is exemplary, given that no one in the game is better at hitting line drives. And for concerned fantasy owners: sure, he's thirty and it makes sense for him to slow down, but the invisible eyes that lace each stadium still think he's one of the faster runners in the game, so factor that into all the other ways that Merrifield remains underrated going into 2020.

YEAR	TEAM	LVL	AGE	PA	DRC+	VORP	BABIP	BRR	FRAA	WARP
2017	OMA	AAA	28	37	169	5.5	.393	-1.3	2B(6): 0.3, RF(1): -0.1	0.3
2017	KCA	MLB	28	630	113	27.2	.308	1.7	2B(132): -0.2, RF(10): -1.9	2.9
2018	KCA	MLB	29	707	119	38.3	.352	3.5	2B(108): 2.3, CF(30): 1.4	4.4
2019	KCA	MLB	30	735	110	30.8	.350	-1.9	2B(82): 6.2, RF(61): -6.4	3.0
2020	KCA	MLB	31	595	95	17.9	.326	0.1	CF 7, 2B 1	2.6

Whit Merrifield, continued

Batted Ball Distribution

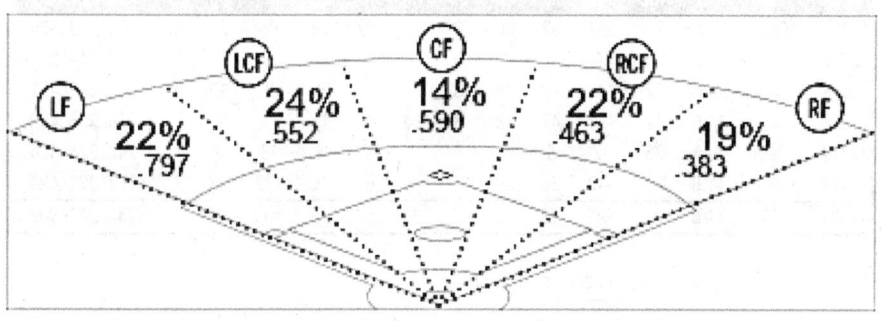

Strike Zone vs LHP   **Strike Zone vs RHP**

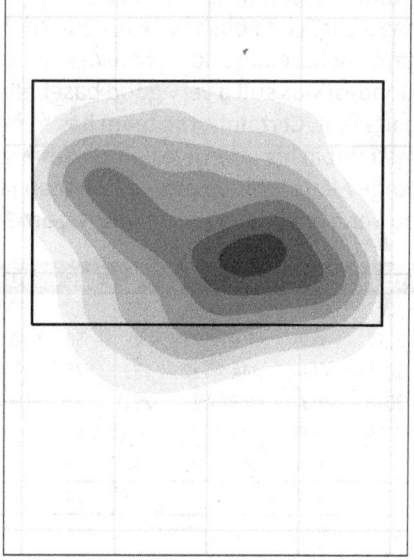

Adalberto Mondesi   SS

Born: 07/27/95   Age: 24   Bats: B   Throws: R
Height: 6'1"   Weight: 190   Origin: International Free Agent, 2011

YEAR	TEAM	LVL	AGE	PA	R	2B	3B	HR	RBI	BB	K	SB	CS	AVG/OBP/SLG
2017	OMA	AAA	21	357	52	20	8	13	52	18	86	21	3	.305/.340/.539
2017	KCA	MLB	21	60	4	1	0	1	3	3	22	5	2	.170/.214/.245
2018	OMA	AAA	22	133	19	8	3	5	21	8	30	10	0	.250/.295/.492
2018	KCA	MLB	22	291	47	13	3	14	37	11	77	32	7	.276/.306/.498
2019	OMA	AAA	23	37	5	1	1	1	3	4	13	2	1	.242/.324/.424
2019	KCA	MLB	23	443	58	20	10	9	62	19	132	43	7	.263/.291/.424
2020	KCA	MLB	24	525	53	23	7	15	59	25	160	32	7	.242/.281/.407

Comparables: Rougned Odor, Ted Lepcio, Javier Báez

As BP author Zach Crizer pointed out, 2019 PECOTA projected Mondesi to hit 15+ home runs, steal 40+ bases and post an OBP below .300, something that no baseball player had ever done before. They still haven't, but only because Mondesi lost time to a groin pull and two shoulder injuries, the second of which has a chance to push back his 2020 debut past Opening Day. It's a credit to the game of baseball and its core design, that despite the flaws and the misfortune Mondesi was still a very good baseball player despite being very bad at certain parts of it. Certainly, the team has to hope that it can introduce some level of restraint in his offensive game—among players with 300 plate appearances, only Jorge Alfaro whiffed more often than Mondesi—his speed, defense and raw power make him a special player, albeit not a perfect one.

YEAR	TEAM	LVL	AGE	PA	DRC+	VORP	BABIP	BRR	FRAA	WARP
2017	OMA	AAA	21	357	107	30.5	.373	1.3	SS(71): 2.2, 2B(10): 0.1	2.2
2017	KCA	MLB	21	60	50	-5.8	.267	-1.4	2B(14): 0.1, SS(9): 0.1	-0.3
2018	OMA	AAA	22	133	75	7.6	.291	1.2	SS(18): 0.6, 2B(6): 0.8	0.4
2018	KCA	MLB	22	291	104	18.4	.335	0.3	SS(61): 1.2, 2B(12): 0.9	1.6
2019	OMA	AAA	23	37	67	1.0	.368	0.5	SS(6): 0.1	0.0
2019	KCA	MLB	23	443	75	7.0	.357	3.1	SS(100): 6.3	1.6
2020	KCA	MLB	24	525	74	2.0	.326	-0.2	SS 6	0.8

Adalberto Mondesi, continued

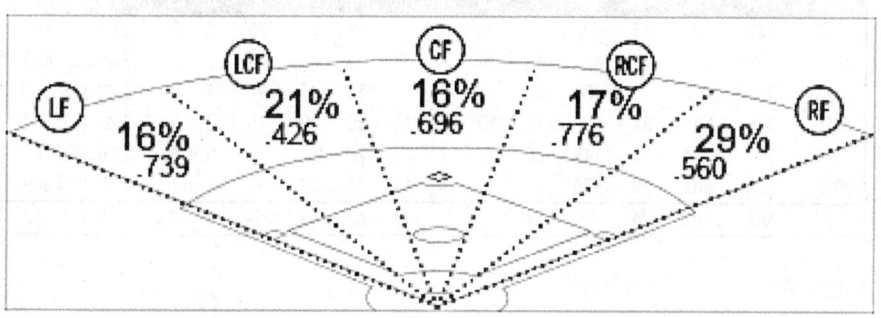

Batted Ball Distribution

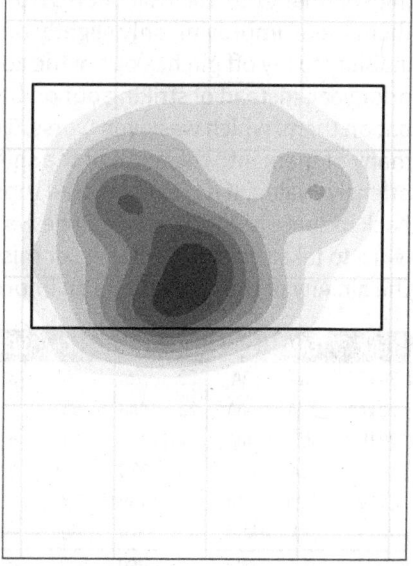

Strike Zone vs LHP

Strike Zone vs RHP

Ryan O'Hearn 1B

Born: 07/26/93 Age: 26 Bats: L Throws: L
Height: 6'3" Weight: 200 Origin: Round 8, 2014 Draft (#243 overall)

YEAR	TEAM	LVL	AGE	PA	R	2B	3B	HR	RBI	BB	K	SB	CS	AVG/OBP/SLG
2017	NWA	AA	23	76	7	1	1	4	11	10	20	0	0	.258/.355/.485
2017	OMA	AAA	23	463	48	26	1	18	53	45	119	1	0	.252/.325/.450
2018	OMA	AAA	24	406	47	21	1	11	52	45	97	2	0	.232/.322/.391
2018	KCA	MLB	24	170	23	10	2	12	30	20	45	0	0	.262/.353/.597
2019	OMA	AAA	25	149	20	10	1	9	28	17	31	0	0	.295/.383/.597
2019	KCA	MLB	25	370	32	13	1	14	38	39	99	0	1	.195/.281/.369
2020	KCA	MLB	26	490	54	23	1	19	62	48	134	1	0	.221/.301/.412

Comparables: Brandon Allen, Greg Bird, Nick Evans

More contact isn't always better contact. It's rare to see a player add five percent to their contact rate and struggle mightily, but O'Hearn was never able to recapture the unexpected brilliance of his 2018 autumn, leading to a midsummer exile. He took out his frustrations on Triple-A pitchers but also left them there, improving only slightly on his return. His downfall was a sudden inability to lay off pitches out of the zone, something he'd done well to avoid the prior year. Instead of striking out on bad pitches, however, he actually got the bat on them, which was even worse. The result was a spike in ground balls, many of them into the teeth of the shift, eroding his power and, with it, his offensive value. If he'd just missed those pitches, he could have at least fought back in some of those counts. If he wants to stick around, O'Hearn will need to learn to take those bad pitches, or miss them, or figure out a way to hit them in the air. Any of those would be an improvement.

YEAR	TEAM	LVL	AGE	PA	DRC+	VORP	BABIP	BRR	FRAA	WARP
2017	NWA	AA	23	76	128	3.3	.310	0.1	1B(8): 0.3, LF(5): -0.6	0.3
2017	OMA	AAA	23	463	95	4.9	.309	-2.5	1B(75): -1.2, RF(5): -0.2	0.0
2018	OMA	AAA	24	406	91	6.0	.286	3.9	1B(69): -6.3, LF(13): -2.1	-0.2
2018	KCA	MLB	24	170	130	8.9	.293	-3.6	1B(31): 0.4, LF(1): -0.1	0.5
2019	OMA	AAA	25	149	130	12.8	.322	0.5	1B(25): 0.0	0.8
2019	KCA	MLB	25	370	80	-3.9	.230	-1.0	1B(94): -5.0, LF(2): -0.1	-1.0
2020	KCA	MLB	26	490	83	-4.0	.271	-2.4	1B -4	-0.8

Ryan O'Hearn, continued

Batted Ball Distribution

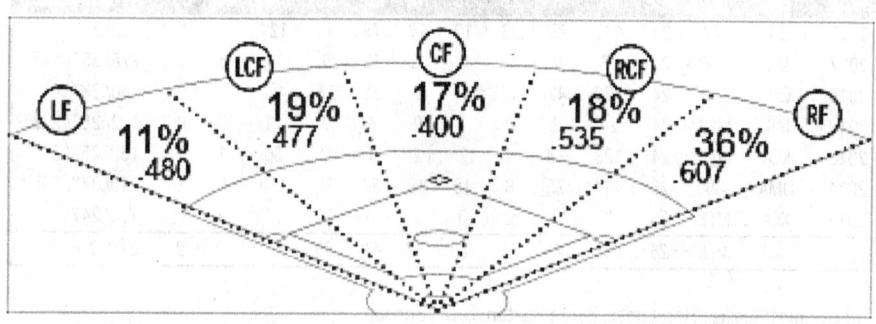

Strike Zone vs LHP   **Strike Zone vs RHP**

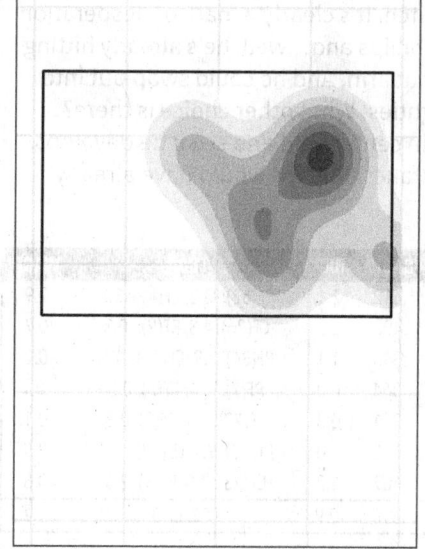
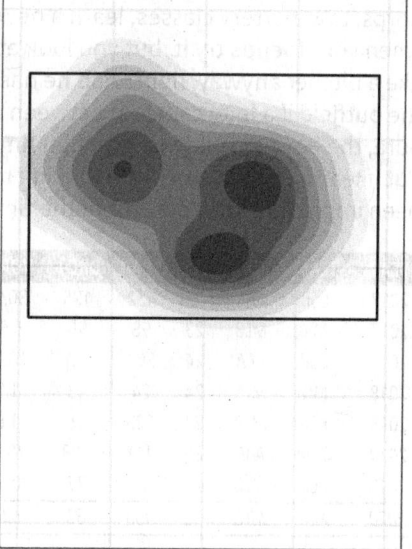

Kansas City Royals 2020

Brett Phillips   OF
Born: 05/30/94   Age: 26   Bats: L   Throws: R
Height: 6'0"   Weight: 185   Origin: Round 6, 2012 Draft (#189 overall)

YEAR	TEAM	LVL	AGE	PA	R	2B	3B	HR	RBI	BB	K	SB	CS	AVG/OBP/SLG
2017	CSP	AAA	23	432	79	23	10	19	78	45	129	9	1	.305/.377/.567
2017	MIL	MLB	23	98	9	3	0	4	12	9	34	5	0	.276/.351/.448
2018	CSP	AAA	24	299	42	12	7	6	25	36	94	11	0	.240/.331/.411
2018	MIL	MLB	24	24	2	0	1	0	4	2	11	0	0	.182/.250/.273
2018	KCA	MLB	24	123	13	4	2	2	7	9	50	1	1	.188/.252/.313
2019	OMA	AAA	25	414	75	8	13	18	54	72	118	22	1	.240/.378/.505
2019	KCA	MLB	25	79	7	2	0	2	6	10	23	3	0	.138/.247/.262
2020	KCA	MLB	26	455	48	19	6	12	50	53	151	9	3	.219/.316/.389

Comparables: Teoscar Hernández, Byron Buxton, Lewis Brinson

The novelty of the two-way player is, admittedly, starting to wear off. It's really just the newest form of the same old lazy swipe at reinvention: move to a new town, quit your job and try acting, change up your batting stance, join the Peace Corps, take pottery classes, learn a new pitch. It's clearly a mark of desperation when your friends try it, but you look at Phillips and…well, he's already hitting like a pitcher anyway, right? And he has that arm. And he could swap out into the outfield if a lefty came up between righties! What other choice is there? Sure, the Royals could just give him time in center field and see if he develops, but if learning just came from making mistakes, Phillips would have already been improving forty percent of the time.

YEAR	TEAM	LVL	AGE	PA	DRC+	VORP	BABIP	BRR	FRAA	WARP
2017	CSP	AAA	23	432	125	30.9	.412	2.1	RF(52): -3.2, CF(49): 3.9	2.9
2017	MIL	MLB	23	98	90	6.5	.408	0.3	CF(26): 4.8, RF(9): -0.3	0.7
2018	CSP	AAA	24	299	77	10.7	.346	1.1	RF(34): 2.9, CF(20): -1.8	0.2
2018	MIL	MLB	24	24	43	-1.0	.364	0.0	RF(7): -0.6, CF(5): 0.5	-0.1
2018	KCA	MLB	24	123	46	-1.8	.311	0.3	CF(23): 4.4, RF(9): 0.3	0.1
2019	OMA	AAA	25	414	108	28.8	.312	3.0	RF(63): 9.4, CF(32): -1.1	2.5
2019	KCA	MLB	25	79	77	0.5	.167	1.2	CF(23): 1.0, RF(3): 2.0	0.5
2020	KCA	MLB	26	455	85	6.0	.318	0.9	LF 2, CF 3	1.1

Brett Phillips, continued

Batted Ball Distribution

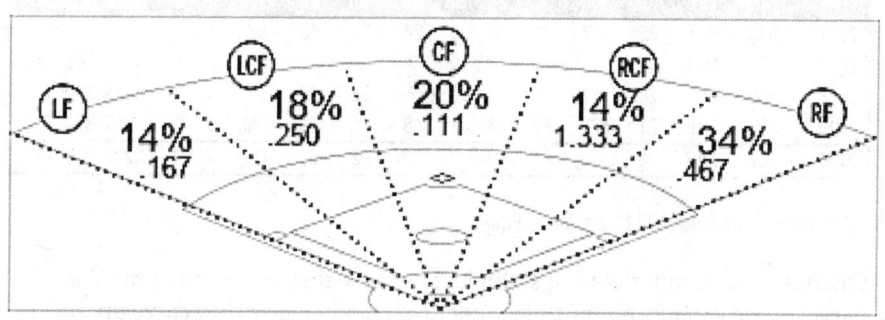

Strike Zone vs LHP   **Strike Zone vs RHP**

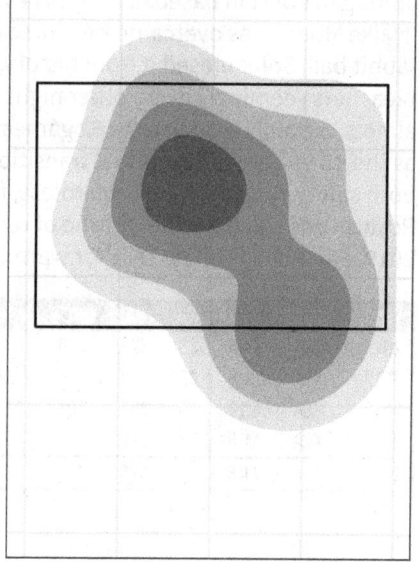

Kansas City Royals 2020

Jorge Soler RF
Born: 02/25/92 Age: 28 Bats: R Throws: R
Height: 6'4" Weight: 230 Origin: International Free Agent, 2012

YEAR	TEAM	LVL	AGE	PA	R	2B	3B	HR	RBI	BB	K	SB	CS	AVG/OBP/SLG
2017	OMA	AAA	25	327	49	9	0	24	59	50	82	1	0	.267/.388/.564
2017	KCA	MLB	25	110	7	5	0	2	6	12	36	0	0	.144/.245/.258
2018	KCA	MLB	26	257	27	18	0	9	28	28	69	3	1	.265/.354/.466
2019	KCA	MLB	27	679	95	33	1	48	117	73	178	3	1	.265/.354/.569
2020	KCA	MLB	28	595	81	27	1	33	92	66	159	3	1	.249/.340/.493

Comparables: Jay Bruce, Wil Myers, Yasiel Puig

Calendars are wonderful things. Not just because they allow us to time our harvests and arrange our business meetings, but because they carve up the endless parade of afternoons into something digestible, relatable, easy to celebrate. Soler's career has been checkered by hamstring injuries and expectations, but for one calendar year, one brief six-month moment, he stood among the best in baseball and was everything Jorge Soler could be all at once. If Mike Moustakas overcame the Curse of Balboni in 2017 with the aid of the rabbit ball, Soler erased it from history, clubbing baseballs deep into the bleachers seemingly every other night. He may never be quite this again—he almost certainly won't start 162 games again, a number almost as unthinkable as the 48—though the gradual transition toward full-time DH is a wise choice for both safety and value. But regardless, for a franchise as deep in winter as the Royals, fans will have the fortune of remembering Soler when they think of 2019, and not a faceless reliever warming up in the fourth.

YEAR	TEAM	LVL	AGE	PA	DRC+	VORP	BABIP	BRR	FRAA	WARP
2017	OMA	AAA	25	327	140	24.9	.293	-2.0	RF(39): -0.4, LF(23): 3.0	2.4
2017	KCA	MLB	25	110	64	-8.6	.203	-0.3	RF(15): -1.6, LF(7): 0.8	-0.4
2018	KCA	MLB	26	257	101	11.6	.340	-0.5	RF(52): -1.0	0.4
2019	KCA	MLB	27	679	142	49.5	.294	-4.3	RF(56): 0.4	4.5
2020	KCA	MLB	28	595	122	21.9	.293	-2.3	RF 0	2.2

Jorge Soler, continued

Batted Ball Distribution

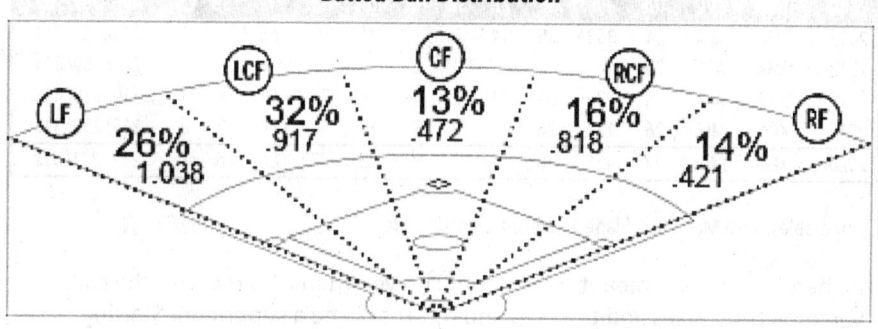

Strike Zone vs LHP   **Strike Zone vs RHP**

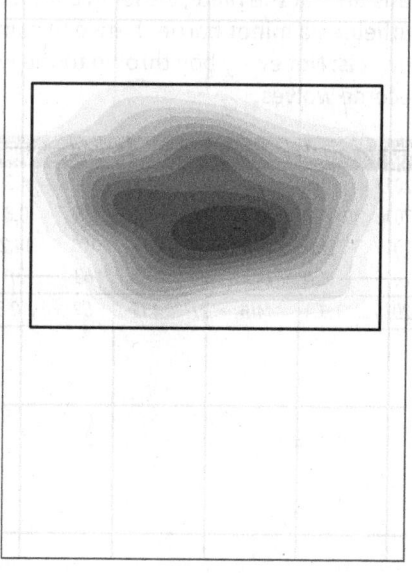

Bubba Starling CF

Born: 08/03/92 Age: 27 Bats: R Throws: R
Height: 6'4" Weight: 215 Origin: Round 1, 2011 Draft (#5 overall)

YEAR	TEAM	LVL	AGE	PA	R	2B	3B	HR	RBI	BB	K	SB	CS	AVG/OBP/SLG
2017	OMA	AAA	24	303	35	14	1	7	21	19	65	5	4	.248/.303/.381
2018	OMA	AAA	25	41	5	2	0	0	2	5	6	1	0	.257/.350/.314
2019	OMA	AAA	26	285	34	11	2	7	38	21	59	9	3	.310/.358/.448
2019	KCA	MLB	26	197	26	7	0	4	12	9	56	2	0	.215/.255/.317
2020	KCA	MLB	27	455	40	17	1	10	43	27	131	6	3	.217/.271/.332

Comparables: Jake Marisnick, Slade Heathcott, Daniel Fields

The hero's journey is meant to be about an everyman who receives the call, overcomes obstacles and tragedy, and returns home a superman. Starling started his path as the superhero and came out the other side an ordinary man. After years of setbacks and struggles, the former fifth-overall pick finally made the majors, and the outcome was anything but storybook. His athleticism never translated at the plate, either in contact or power, and now he's a spare outfielder, a minor barrier between some other young man and glory. That's just how it is: Not every boy thrown to the wolves becomes a hero. Most of them just become wolves.

YEAR	TEAM	LVL	AGE	PA	DRC+	VORP	BABIP	BRR	FRAA	WARP
2017	OMA	AAA	24	303	81	1.3	.301	-2.2	RF(40): 7.7, CF(37): 3.4	1.0
2018	OMA	AAA	25	41	88	0.8	.310	-0.2	CF(10): -0.7, RF(1): -0.1	0.0
2019	OMA	AAA	26	285	101	14.2	.374	0.0	CF(51): 3.1, RF(18): 2.2	1.4
2019	KCA	MLB	26	197	63	-3.1	.286	3.8	CF(36): 5.8, RF(23): -0.4	0.5
2020	KCA	MLB	27	455	59	-10.8	.291	0.0	LF -4, CF 1	-1.3

Bubba Starling, continued

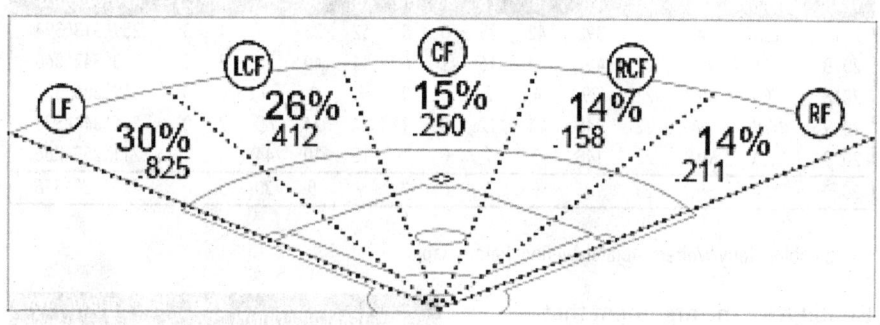

Batted Ball Distribution

Strike Zone vs LHP **Strike Zone vs RHP**

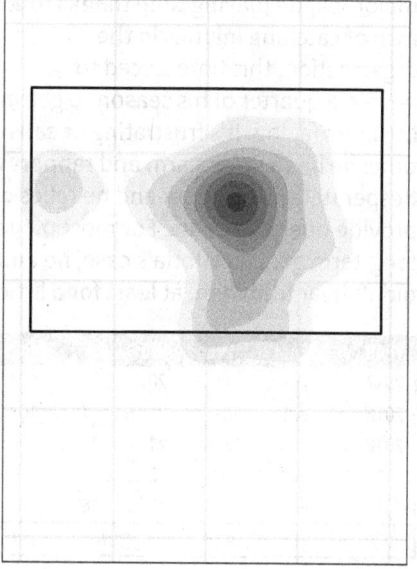

Meibrys Viloria C

Born: 02/15/97   Age: 23   Bats: L   Throws: R
Height: 5'11"   Weight: 220   Origin: International Free Agent, 2013

YEAR	TEAM	LVL	AGE	PA	R	2B	3B	HR	RBI	BB	K	SB	CS	AVG/OBP/SLG
2017	LEX	A	20	398	42	25	0	8	52	25	79	4	3	.259/.313/.394
2018	WIL	A+	21	407	34	16	1	6	44	40	75	2	1	.260/.342/.360
2018	KCA	MLB	21	29	4	2	0	0	4	1	9	0	0	.259/.286/.333
2019	NWA	AA	22	248	21	12	0	1	24	24	60	2	0	.264/.344/.332
2019	KCA	MLB	22	148	7	7	0	1	15	10	44	0	1	.211/.259/.286
2020	KCA	MLB	23	105	9	5	0	1	9	8	30	0	0	.226/.288/.318

Comparables: Tony Wolters, Abiatal Avelino, Raimel Tapia

Exhibit A for the argument that baseball games are actually detrimental to rebuilding franchises, Viloria was once again thrust into major-league playing time thanks to a rash of catching injuries in the organization, this time forced to devote a quarter of his season to getting battered around by pitchers he had no business facing. It's frustrating because Viloria could really use the development time: he has a strong arm and rapport with his pitchers, but his framing desperately needs work and he relies on the always-capricious hit tool to provide offensive value. For most players, being in the majors is the short- and long-term goal; in Viloria's case, he and the Royals would both be better off if we didn't hear from him, at least for a little while.

YEAR	TEAM	P. COUNT	FRM RUNS	BLK RUNS	THRW RUNS	TOT RUNS
2018	KCA	1167	0.0	-0.8	0.0	-0.1
2019	KCA	5921	-4.0	0.0	0.3	-3.2
2019	NWA	8242	-7.7	0.0	0.3	-7.7
2020	KCA	4022	-1.4	-0.4	0.3	-1.5

YEAR	TEAM	LVL	AGE	PA	DRC+	VORP	BABIP	BRR	FRAA	WARP
2017	LEX	A	20	398	104	8.2	.310	-0.4	C(92): -0.4	1.8
2018	WIL	A+	21	407	107	11.0	.313	-2.8	C(88): 2.8	2.1
2018	KCA	MLB	21	29	74	0.2	.389	0.1	C(10): -1.0	0.0
2019	NWA	AA	22	248	97	9.2	.358	0.9	C(58): -6.3	0.5
2019	KCA	MLB	22	148	59	-0.1	.293	-0.5	C(41): -3.6	-0.4
2020	KCA	MLB	23	105	58	-1.1	.311	-0.2	C -2	-0.3

Meibrys Viloria, continued

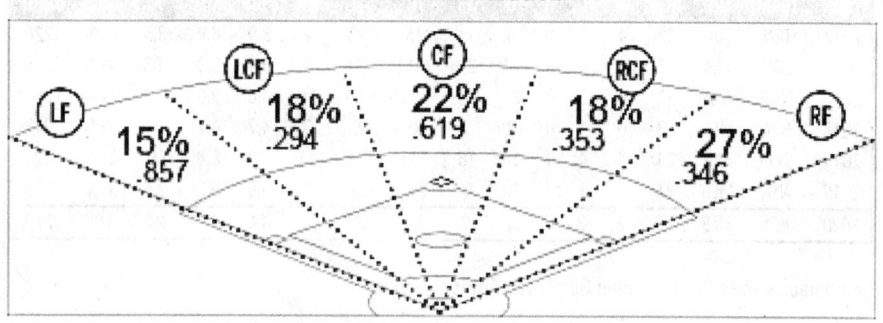

Batted Ball Distribution

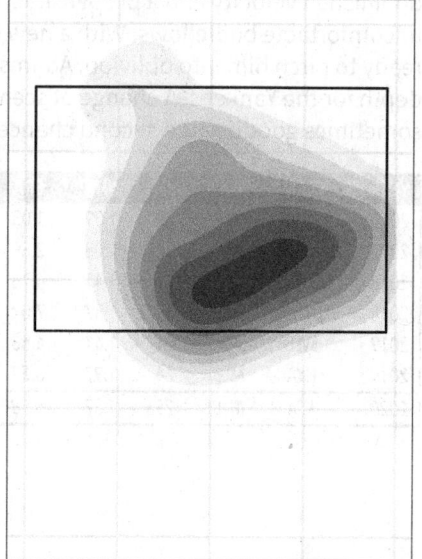

Strike Zone vs LHP *Strike Zone vs RHP*

Chance Adams   RHP

Born: 08/10/94   Age: 25   Bats: R   Throws: R
Height: 6'1"   Weight: 225   Origin: Round 5, 2015 Draft (#153 overall)

YEAR	TEAM	LVL	AGE	W	L	SV	G	GS	IP	H	HR	BB/9	K/9	K	GB%	BABIP
2017	TRN	AA	22	4	0	0	6	6	35	23	2	3.9	8.2	32	43%	.228
2017	SWB	AAA	22	11	5	0	21	21	115^1	81	9	3.4	8.0	103	42%	.236
2018	SWB	AAA	23	4	5	0	27	23	113	101	16	4.6	9.0	113	42%	.282
2018	NYA	MLB	23	0	1	0	3	1	7^2	8	3	4.7	4.7	4	38%	.217
2019	SWB	AAA	24	4	4	1	18	15	81^2	77	11	4.2	8.8	80	37%	.291
2019	NYA	MLB	24	1	1	1	13	0	25^1	39	7	3.9	8.2	23	31%	.395
2020	KCA	MLB	25	2	2	0	33	0	35	39	7	4.0	6.1	24	35%	.293

Comparables: Jake Faria, Stephen Gonsalves, Anthony Banda

Once upon a time, Adams was a promising prospect. That time has long since passed, and Adams has just about run out of chances. A spot in the starting rotation was his for the taking and he let it slip through his hands as his diminished velocity and a propensity for allowing fly balls made for uncomfortable bedfellows. With a new batch of hard-throwing minor leaguers ready to pitch him into oblivion, Adams has become little more than necessary depth for the Yankees. A change of scenery might be just what he needs, as sometimes goodbye is a second chance.

YEAR	TEAM	LVL	AGE	WHIP	ERA	DRA	WARP	MPH	FB%	WHF	CSP
2017	TRN	AA	22	1.09	1.03	2.84	1.0				
2017	SWB	AAA	22	1.08	2.89	2.90	3.5				
2018	SWB	AAA	23	1.41	4.78	4.86	0.9				
2018	NYA	MLB	23	1.57	7.04	7.07	-0.2	94.4	66.7	5.2	41.6
2019	SWB	AAA	24	1.41	4.63	4.19	2.0				
2019	NYA	MLB	24	1.97	8.53	8.77	-0.9	93.6	58.8	8.3	43.5
2020	KCA	MLB	25	1.57	5.98	5.89	-0.3	93.5	61.7	7.9	43.7

Chance Adams, continued

Pitch Shape vs LHH

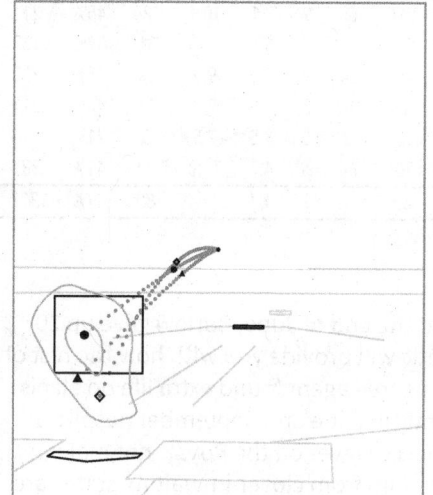

Pitch Shape vs RHH

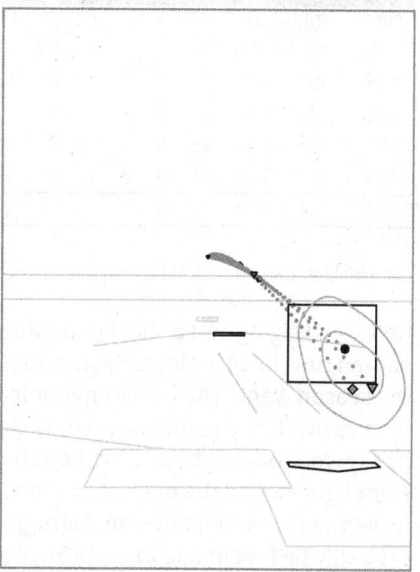

Type	Frequency	Velocity	H Movement	V Movement
● Fastball	58.8%	91.8 [98]	-3.7 [114]	-15.5 [101]
☐ Sinker				
+ Cutter				
▲ Changeup	7.1%	85.7 [102]	-12.4 [94]	-25.3 [106]
✕ Splitter				
▽ Slider	15.6%	83.6 [97]	8.2 [113]	-35 [95]
◇ Curveball	18.5%	79.3 [102]	15.1 [131]	-44.8 [106]
✦ Slow Curveball				
✱ Knuckleball				
▼ Screwball				

Scott Barlow   RHP

Born: 12/18/92   Age: 27   Bats: R   Throws: R
Height: 6'3"   Weight: 215   Origin: Round 6, 2011 Draft (#194 overall)

YEAR	TEAM	LVL	AGE	W	L	SV	G	GS	IP	H	HR	BB/9	K/9	K	GB%	BABIP
2017	TUL	AA	24	6	3	0	19	19	107^1	60	9	3.1	10.4	124	45%	.211
2017	OKL	AAA	24	1	3	0	7	7	32^1	37	6	6.4	10.0	36	37%	.333
2018	OMA	AAA	25	1	4	1	13	10	45^2	54	9	4.1	9.9	50	38%	.357
2018	KCA	MLB	25	1	1	0	6	0	15	16	2	1.8	9.0	15	40%	.311
2019	OMA	AAA	26	0	0	1	3	0	6	3	0	4.5	7.5	5	21%	.214
2019	KCA	MLB	26	3	3	1	61	0	70^1	64	6	4.7	11.8	92	41%	.337
2020	KCA	MLB	27	3	3	3	60	0	63	54	7	4.1	11.4	80	41%	.307

Comparables: Chris Ellis, Paul Clemens, Adrian Houser

Between May 25 and a short demotion at the end of June, Barlow gave up 20 earned runs in 14 innings. Basic arithmetic will provide you with how the rest of the season went. The former minor league free agent found extra life on all his pitches in 2019, wearing down only slightly in June and September despite a heavy workload. At this point, he's the best reliever on the Royals not making eight figures, and the only issues keeping him from closer-in-waiting status are flickering command and some struggles against lefties with the slider. He'll probably be first in line to close anyway, once Ian Kennedy gets shipped off or becomes Ian Kennedy again.

YEAR	TEAM	LVL	AGE	WHIP	ERA	DRA	WARP	MPH	FB%	WHF	CSP
2017	TUL	AA	24	0.90	2.10	2.57	3.3				
2017	OKL	AAA	24	1.86	7.24	5.39	0.1				
2018	OMA	AAA	25	1.64	6.11	5.78	-0.1				
2018	KCA	MLB	25	1.27	3.60	3.69	0.2	93.6	53	11.9	50.8
2019	OMA	AAA	26	1.00	0.00	4.01	0.1				
2019	KCA	MLB	26	1.44	4.22	4.20	0.9	96.6	43.5	15.7	44.4
2020	KCA	MLB	27	1.31	3.85	3.84	0.9	95.7	45.2	15.4	47.8

Scott Barlow, continued

Pitch Shape vs LHH

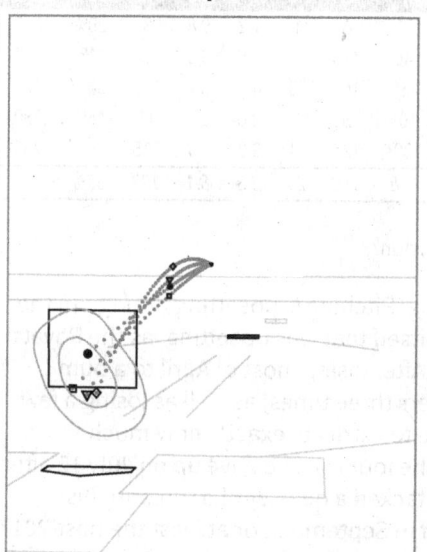

Pitch Shape vs RHH

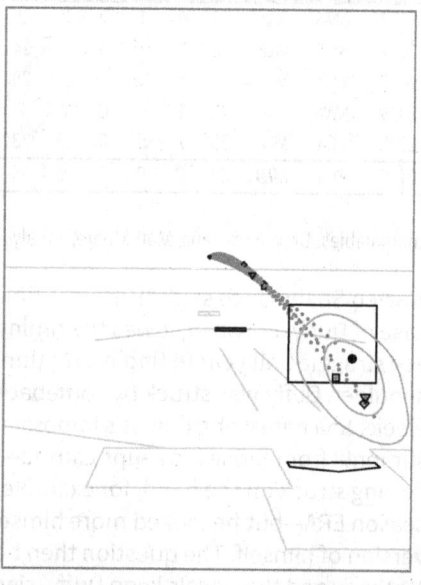

Type	Frequency	Velocity	H Movement	V Movement
● Fastball	35.3%	94.8 [107]	-3.3 [116]	-14.5 [104]
□ Sinker	8.2%	94.2 [108]	-11.4 [108]	-20.3 [100]
+ Cutter				
▲ Changeup				
✕ Splitter				
▽ Slider	43.6%	84.2 [99]	7.8 [112]	-37.1 [88]
◇ Curveball	12.8%	77.7 [97]	13.7 [125]	-51.4 [92]
⊕ Slow Curveball				
✱ Knuckleball				
▼ Screwball				

Danny Duffy LHP

Born: 12/21/88 Age: 31 Bats: L Throws: L
Height: 6'3" Weight: 205 Origin: Round 3, 2007 Draft (#96 overall)

YEAR	TEAM	LVL	AGE	W	L	SV	G	GS	IP	H	HR	BB/9	K/9	K	GB%	BABIP
2017	OMA	AAA	28	0	1	0	2	2	7^1	6	1	1.2	9.8	8	30%	.263
2017	KCA	MLB	28	9	10	0	24	24	146^1	143	13	2.5	8.0	130	41%	.309
2018	KCA	MLB	29	8	12	0	28	28	155	161	23	4.1	8.2	141	36%	.304
2019	NWA	AA	30	1	0	0	2	2	10^1	8	1	0.0	9.6	11	46%	.280
2019	KCA	MLB	30	7	6	0	23	23	130^2	125	21	3.2	7.9	115	36%	.285
2020	KCA	MLB	31	9	9	0	26	26	148	150	24	3.3	8.1	133	35%	.298

Comparables: Drew Pomeranz, Matt Moore, Jhoulys Chacín

Warren Spahn once said: "Hitting is timing. Pitching is upsetting timing." In the case of Duffy, however, it was the timing itself that was upsetting, as the Royals' ace struggled all year to find his rhythm. After losing most of April to a bum shoulder, Duffy was struck by comebackers three times, as well as losing a few weeks to a hamstring pull. It's impossible to extricate exactly how much shrapnel from those blow-ups caused—the four runs he gave up on July 12 after getting struck on the hand, for example, tacked a quarter of a run onto his season ERA—but he looked more himself in September, or at least the post-2017 version of himself. The question then becomes whether new manager Mike Matheny and the Royals keep Duffy, signed through 2021, on board for his veteran leadership, or whether they trade him to make room for the new wave. It may come down to his value, and the timing.

YEAR	TEAM	LVL	AGE	WHIP	ERA	DRA	WARP	MPH	FB%	WHF	CSP
2017	OMA	AAA	28	0.95	3.68	3.18	0.2				
2017	KCA	MLB	28	1.26	3.81	3.87	2.8	95.2	47.3	12.3	50.6
2018	KCA	MLB	29	1.49	4.88	5.54	-0.4	95.8	55.7	10.8	49.6
2019	NWA	AA	30	0.77	0.87	3.24	0.2				
2019	KCA	MLB	30	1.31	4.34	5.35	0.6	94.8	53	11.4	51
2020	KCA	MLB	31	1.38	4.81	4.78	1.3	94.4	52.4	11.3	50.1

Danny Duffy, continued

Pitch Shape vs LHH

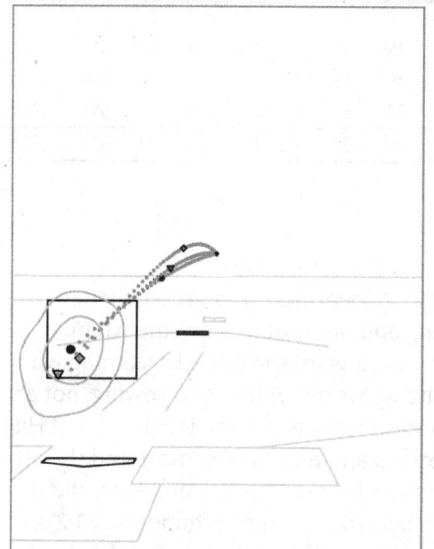

Pitch Shape vs RHH

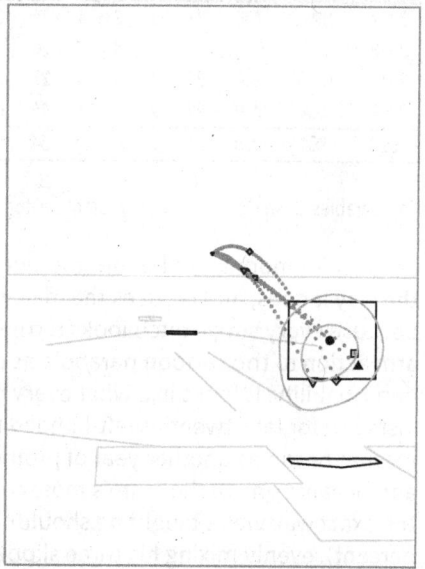

Type	Frequency	Velocity	H Movement	V Movement
● Fastball	44.8%	92.8 [101]	6.7 [101]	-12.7 [108]
☐ Sinker	8.2%	92.5 [99]	11.8 [106]	-15.8 [116]
+ Cutter				
▲ Changeup	11.6%	84.2 [96]	13.6 [89]	-24.2 [109]
✕ Splitter				
▽ Slider	26.4%	84.4 [100]	-2.5 [90]	-32.9 [101]
◇ Curveball	9.0%	76.6 [93]	-7.3 [99]	-55.8 [83]
✦ Slow Curveball				
✱ Knuckleball				
▼ Screwball				

Tim Hill LHP

Born: 02/10/90   Age: 30   Bats: R   Throws: L
Height: 6'2"   Weight: 200   Origin: Round 32, 2014 Draft (#963 overall)

YEAR	TEAM	LVL	AGE	W	L	SV	G	GS	IP	H	HR	BB/9	K/9	K	GB%	BABIP
2017	NWA	AA	27	1	2	4	36	0	69	76	2	2.5	9.8	75	62%	.372
2018	KCA	MLB	28	1	4	2	70	0	45^2	46	4	2.8	8.3	42	64%	.309
2019	OMA	AAA	29	1	1	3	27	0	29^2	26	2	1.8	9.1	30	55%	.308
2019	KCA	MLB	29	2	0	1	46	0	39^2	31	4	2.9	8.8	39	58%	.267
2020	KCA	MLB	30	3	3	0	54	0	57	59	9	2.6	7.6	48	57%	.298

Comparables: Josh Osich, Ryan Kelly, Grant Dayton

Let's take a moment to lament the sidearmer. It's a shame that physics works the way it does, and reduces the majority of sidearmers to platoon pitchers, because every single pitch looks terrifying and unhittable, from the whiplike arm action to the cartoon parabola as it rises toward the plate, screaming with improbability. It looks like what every pitcher would dream of throwing, not a last gasp for late-twenties left-handed non-prospects. So it's delightful that Hill, in what began as another year of promotions and demotions, mastered the art and became one of the team's most consistent arms after the break. He did it the exact way we're taught he shouldn't: by striking out righthanders (29.2 percent), evenly mixing his three slippery pitches (fastball, sinker, slider) in equal measure. Quiz would be proud.

YEAR	TEAM	LVL	AGE	WHIP	ERA	DRA	WARP	MPH	FB%	WHF	CSP
2017	NWA	AA	27	1.38	4.17	4.24	0.5				
2018	KCA	MLB	28	1.31	4.53	5.00	0.0	93.5	76.4	9.5	55.6
2019	OMA	AAA	29	1.08	2.12	2.15	1.2				
2019	KCA	MLB	29	1.11	3.63	3.64	0.7	92.3	75.3	9.7	54.3
2020	KCA	MLB	30	1.32	4.53	4.59	0.4	92.1	75.6	9.6	54.7

Tim Hill, continued

Pitch Shape vs LHH   **Pitch Shape vs RHH**

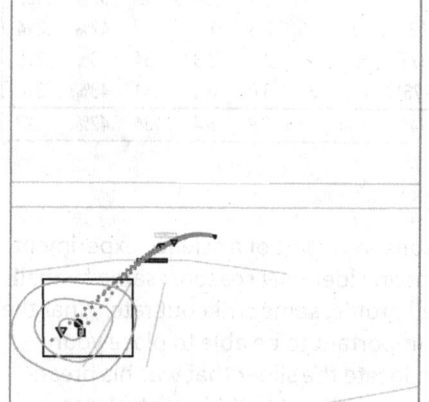
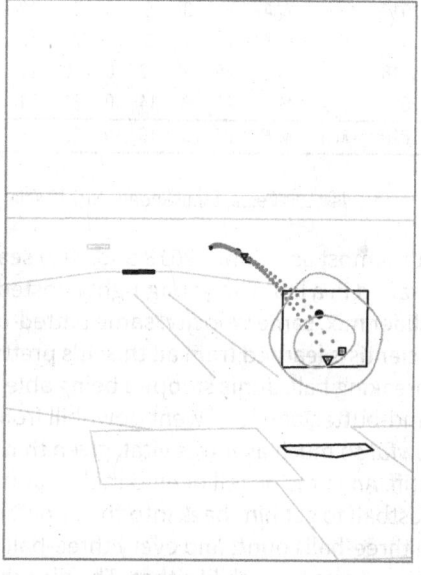

Type	Frequency	Velocity	H Movement	V Movement
● Fastball	30.2%	90.8 [95]	15.7 [61]	-28.1 [68]
☐ Sinker	45.2%	90.3 [88]	13.1 [97]	-34.7 [50]
+ Cutter				
▲ Changeup				
✕ Splitter				
▽ Slider	24.7%	78.3 [74]	-3.2 [92]	-34.3 [97]
◇ Curveball				
✦ Slow Curveball				
✱ Knuckleball				
▼ Screwball				

Royals Player Analysis - 55

Kansas City Royals 2020

Jakob Junis   RHP

Born: 09/16/92   Age: 27   Bats: R   Throws: R
Height: 6'2"   Weight: 225   Origin: Round 29, 2011 Draft (#876 overall)

YEAR	TEAM	LVL	AGE	W	L	SV	G	GS	IP	H	HR	BB/9	K/9	K	GB%	BABIP
2017	OMA	AAA	24	3	5	0	12	12	71	61	6	1.9	10.9	86	37%	.307
2017	KCA	MLB	24	9	3	0	20	16	98¹	101	15	2.3	7.3	80	42%	.294
2018	KCA	MLB	25	9	12	0	30	30	177	182	32	2.2	8.3	164	43%	.298
2019	KCA	MLB	26	9	14	0	31	31	175¹	192	31	3.0	8.4	164	43%	.318
2020	KCA	MLB	27	8	10	0	26	26	145	160	24	2.9	8.4	136	42%	.323

Comparables: Luis Cessa, Esmil Rogers, Nick Pivetta

It's almost as if Junis' 2018 and 2019 seasons were part of a science experiment crafted in a lab. The young righty posted nearly identical seasons: same fastball-slider mix, same velocity, same batted-ball profile, same strikeout rate. What the scientists learned from all this: It's pretty important to be able to place your breaking ball. Junis stopped being able to locate the slider that was his bread-and-butter, and it all went downhill from there. It's not that his control was *awful* so much as it was vital, given that his fastball has always been relatively stiff. Any time he fell behind in the count with errant sliders, he couldn't trust his fastball to get him back into the at-bat. In essence, every two-ball count felt like a three-ball count, and every three-ball count was as good as a walk; it's hard for anyone to pitch like that. The nice thing about mysterious disappearances is that they allow for mysterious reappearances; the team has no reason not to give Junis a chance to lodge the keystone back in place and pitch another set of competent starts.

YEAR	TEAM	LVL	AGE	WHIP	ERA	DRA	WARP	MPH	FB%	WHF	CSP
2017	OMA	AAA	24	1.07	2.92	1.95	2.9				
2017	KCA	MLB	24	1.28	4.30	4.88	0.7	93.5	55.3	9.9	51.8
2018	KCA	MLB	25	1.27	4.37	5.53	-0.4	93.5	53.3	10.3	49.2
2019	KCA	MLB	26	1.43	5.24	5.91	-0.3	93.7	50.8	10.3	47.6
2020	KCA	MLB	27	1.43	5.23	5.10	0.8	93.1	53.1	10.4	49.7

Jakob Junis, continued

Pitch Shape vs LHH

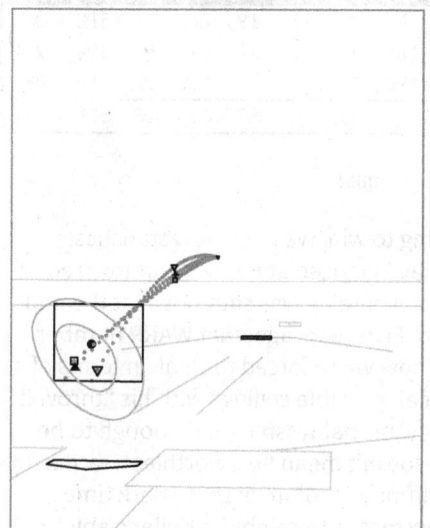

Pitch Shape vs RHH

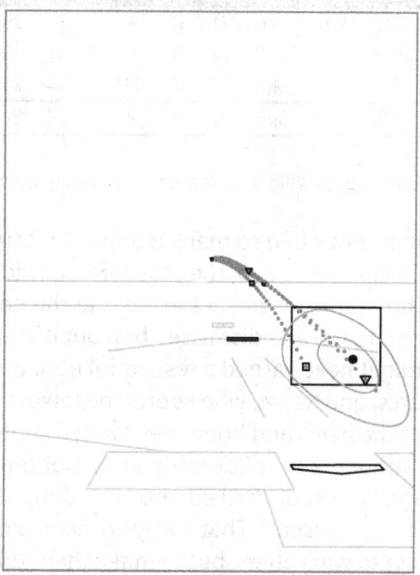

Type	Frequency	Velocity	H Movement	V Movement
● Fastball	34.1%	92.1 [99]	-5 [108]	-16.2 [99]
☐ Sinker	16.7%	91.5 [94]	-11.2 [109]	-21 [98]
+ Cutter				
▲ Changeup	5.3%	85 [99]	-3.8 [134]	-29 [95]
✕ Splitter				
▽ Slider	43.9%	81.8 [89]	13.1 [134]	-38.1 [86]
◇ Curveball				
⊕ Slow Curveball				
✳ Knuckleball				
▼ Screwball				

Brad Keller RHP

Born: 07/27/95   Age: 24   Bats: R   Throws: R
Height: 6'5"   Weight: 230   Origin: Round 8, 2013 Draft (#240 overall)

YEAR	TEAM	LVL	AGE	W	L	SV	G	GS	IP	H	HR	BB/9	K/9	K	GB%	BABIP
2017	WTN	AA	21	10	9	0	26	26	130^2	142	7	3.9	7.6	111	51%	.339
2018	KCA	MLB	22	9	6	0	41	20	140^1	133	7	3.2	6.2	96	56%	.294
2019	KCA	MLB	23	7	14	0	28	28	165^1	154	15	3.8	6.6	122	51%	.282
2020	KCA	MLB	24	8	9	0	24	24	141	152	16	3.7	6.9	108	51%	.310

Comparables: Antonio Senzatela, Jason Adam, German Márquez

In an era when so many teams aren't trying to win, we need new statistics. Twenty years ago, the casual fan would have glanced at Keller's win-loss record (he led the league in the latter at the point where he was shut down at the end of August) and dismissed him out of hand. Five years ago, that WARP number might have earned a respectful nod. But now we're forced to think in terms of arcs, and Keller, who sports the lowest of all possible ceilings with his "throw it at the heels and hope they swing" strategy, probably isn't good enough to be part of the next Royals dynasty. But that doesn't mean he's worthless; rather, for the poor souls tricked into attending Kauffman Stadium in these dark times, he's a godsend. That's why we need a new metric to celebrate Keller's ability, not to win games, but to make them tolerable. "Keller's starting today," you might note. "We might get seven innings out of this game before it gets out of hand." Let's put that on the back of a baseball card.

YEAR	TEAM	LVL	AGE	WHIP	ERA	DRA	WARP	MPH	FB%	WHF	CSP
2017	WTN	AA	21	1.52	4.68	6.07	-1.4				
2018	KCA	MLB	22	1.30	3.08	4.87	0.6	96.5	69.8	9.8	46.5
2019	KCA	MLB	23	1.35	4.19	5.01	1.4	96.2	66.7	9.1	45.7
2020	KCA	MLB	24	1.49	5.00	4.77	1.3	96.1	69.9	9.6	47.5

Brad Keller, continued

Pitch Shape vs LHH

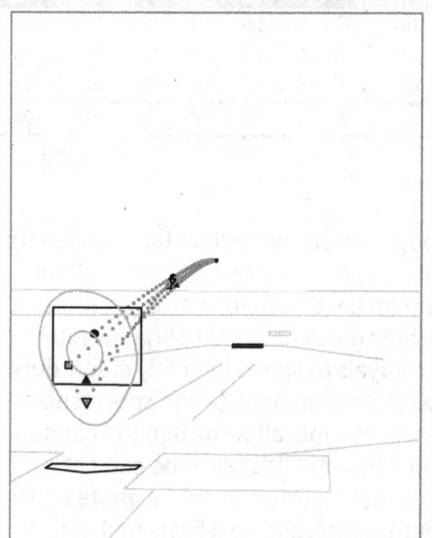

Pitch Shape vs RHH

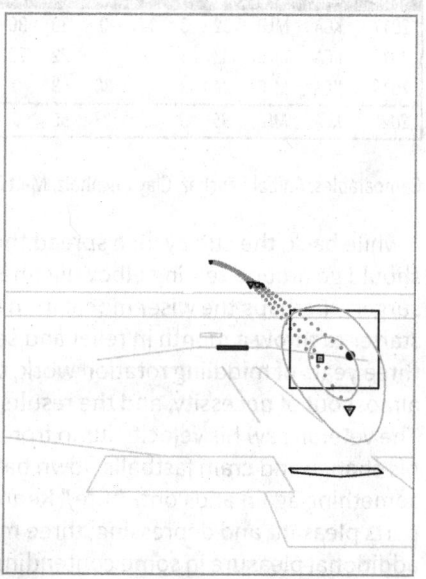

Type	Frequency	Velocity	H Movement	V Movement
● Fastball	41.9%	94.2 [105]	0.2 [131]	-14.8 [103]
☐ Sinker	24.8%	93.4 [104]	-9.3 [122]	-19.1 [104]
+ Cutter				
▲ Changeup				
✕ Splitter				
▽ Slider	31.4%	85.4 [104]	6.4 [106]	-37.2 [88]
◇ Curveball				
⬙ Slow Curveball				
✳ Knuckleball				
▼ Screwball				

Ian Kennedy RHP

Born: 12/19/84 Age: 35 Bats: R Throws: R
Height: 6'0" Weight: 205 Origin: Round 1, 2006 Draft (#21 overall)

YEAR	TEAM	LVL	AGE	W	L	SV	G	GS	IP	H	HR	BB/9	K/9	K	GB%	BABIP
2017	KCA	MLB	32	5	13	0	30	30	154	143	34	3.6	7.7	131	36%	.257
2018	KCA	MLB	33	3	9	0	22	22	119^2	125	20	3.0	7.9	105	31%	.298
2019	KCA	MLB	34	3	2	30	63	0	63^1	64	6	2.4	10.4	73	46%	.343
2020	KCA	MLB	35	3	3	27	60	0	63	63	10	3.0	9.4	66	39%	.308

Comparables: Aníbal Sánchez, Clay Buchholz, Matt Garza

A while back, the cutesy idea spread through certain circles that baseball teams should go around tearing elbow ligaments, given the success of Tommy John surgery. Perhaps the wiser inoculation should have been to force every Triple-A starter to throw a month in relief and see how much their stuff plays up. After three years of middling rotation work, the Royals assigned Kennedy closer duty almost out of necessity, and the results were both immediate and spectacular. The veteran saw his velocity jump from 91 to 95 mph, allowing him to abandon his change and cram fastballs down batters' throats. "It's fun to be good at something again and contribute," Kennedy told reporters in July, a quote equal parts pleasant and depressing; three months more, and he'll likely find additional pleasure in some contending team's pennant run.

YEAR	TEAM	LVL	AGE	WHIP	ERA	DRA	WARP	MPH	FB%	WHF	CSP
2017	KCA	MLB	32	1.32	5.38	6.18	-1.0	93.9	61.7	10.2	50.2
2018	KCA	MLB	33	1.38	4.66	5.32	0.0	94.2	58.7	9	49.2
2019	KCA	MLB	34	1.28	3.41	3.52	1.3	96.2	67.5	11.7	51.6
2020	KCA	MLB	35	1.33	4.41	4.45	0.5	93.4	60.9	9.9	49.6

Ian Kennedy, continued

Pitch Shape vs LHH

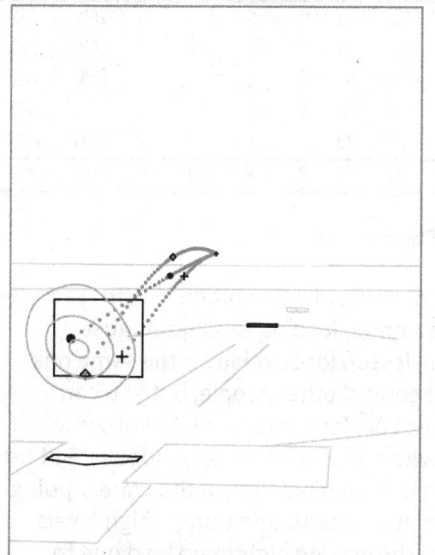

Pitch Shape vs RHH

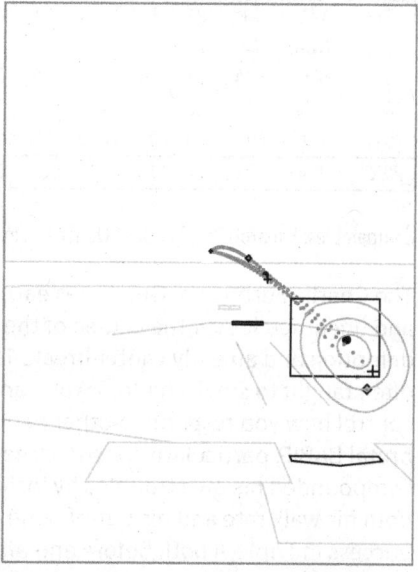

Type	Frequency	Velocity	H Movement	V Movement
● Fastball	67.5%	94.9 [107]	-8.7 [92]	-13 [108]
☐ Sinker				
+ Cutter	15.5%	91.7 [119]	0.1 [90]	-20.7 [112]
▲ Changeup				
✕ Splitter				
▽ Slider				
◇ Curveball	15.2%	81 [108]	10.7 [113]	-49.5 [96]
⊕ Slow Curveball				
✳ Knuckleball				
▼ Screwball				

Richard Lovelady   LHP

Born: 07/07/95   Age: 24   Bats: L   Throws: L
Height: 6'0"   Weight: 175   Origin: Round 10, 2016 Draft (#313 overall)

YEAR	TEAM	LVL	AGE	W	L	SV	G	GS	IP	H	HR	BB/9	K/9	K	GB%	BABIP
2017	WIL	A+	21	1	0	7	21	0	33^1	18	0	1.1	11.1	41	70%	.237
2017	NWA	AA	21	3	2	3	21	0	33^1	28	1	3.5	9.7	36	50%	.310
2018	OMA	AAA	22	3	3	9	46	0	73	53	3	2.6	8.8	71	51%	.262
2019	OMA	AAA	23	1	2	4	24	0	26^1	26	1	2.4	9.9	29	57%	.342
2019	KCA	MLB	23	0	3	0	25	0	20	30	2	3.6	7.7	17	53%	.412
2020	KCA	MLB	24	1	1	0	11	0	11	13	2	2.8	6.4	8	50%	.305

Comparables: Eduardo Paredes, José Quijada, Alex Claudio

The Charlie Furbush of Our Times earned a major league promotion in spring and unearned it over the course of the summer, leading to a late-August demotion and an early winter break. The lesson for Lovelady is the same one often taught to small children: You can't control other people, but you can control how you respond to other people. Lovelady was the victim of some brutal BABIP, particularly for someone who draws so many groundballs. But he compounded his own troubles by losing faith and nibbling at the plate, upping both his walk rate and his out-of-zone contact rate to unnaturally high levels. Success in Triple-A both before and after the waking nightmare lead one to believe that a new year, and renewed confidence, can return Lovelady and his low-slot fastball/slider combo to the rare tier of left-handed relief prospectdom he so recently held.

YEAR	TEAM	LVL	AGE	WHIP	ERA	DRA	WARP	MPH	FB%	WHF	CSP
2017	WIL	A+	21	0.66	1.08	1.86	1.2				
2017	NWA	AA	21	1.23	2.16	3.28	0.6				
2018	OMA	AAA	22	1.01	2.47	2.32	2.3				
2019	OMA	AAA	23	1.25	3.08	1.86	1.1				
2019	KCA	MLB	23	1.90	7.65	5.62	-0.1	96.0	60.8	8.3	53
2020	KCA	MLB	24	1.43	5.04	4.96	0.0	95.8	62.6	8.5	54.6

Richard Lovelady, continued

Pitch Shape vs LHH

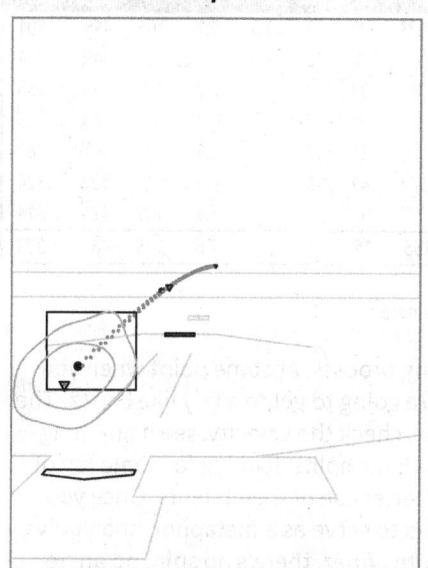

Pitch Shape vs RHH

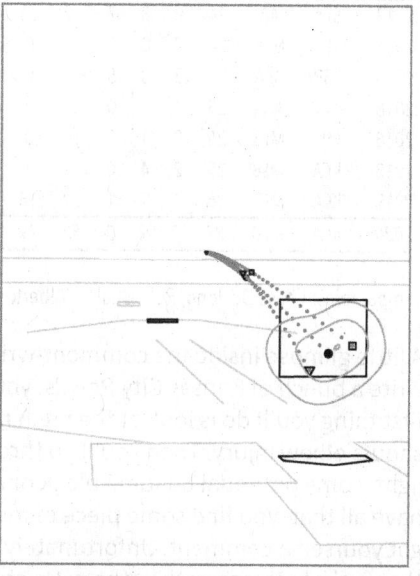

Type	Frequency	Velocity	H Movement	V Movement
● Fastball	47.5%	94.1 [105]	7.4 [97]	-17.5 [96]
□ Sinker	13.3%	94.6 [110]	11.8 [106]	-20.9 [98]
+ Cutter				
▲ Changeup				
✕ Splitter				
▽ Slider	38.9%	87.8 [114]	-3.4 [93]	-26.7 [119]
◇ Curveball				
✥ Slow Curveball				
✱ Knuckleball				
▼ Screwball				

Kansas City Royals 2020

Jorge López RHP

Born: 02/10/93 Age: 27 Bats: R Throws: R
Height: 6'3" Weight: 195 Origin: Round 2, 2011 Draft (#70 overall)

YEAR	TEAM	LVL	AGE	W	L	SV	G	GS	IP	H	HR	BB/9	K/9	K	GB%	BABIP
2017	BLX	AA	24	8	8	7	39	13	103^2	92	7	3.3	9.1	105	49%	.301
2017	MIL	MLB	24	0	0	0	1	0	2	4	0	4.5	0.0	0	44%	.444
2018	CSP	AAA	25	3	3	5	24	0	28^2	33	3	3.1	7.2	23	63%	.333
2018	OMA	AAA	25	1	0	0	2	2	9	8	2	1.0	11.0	11	26%	.286
2018	MIL	MLB	25	0	1	0	10	0	19^2	16	1	5.9	6.9	15	56%	.268
2018	KCA	MLB	25	2	4	0	7	7	34	41	5	2.4	6.1	23	40%	.324
2019	KCA	MLB	26	4	9	1	39	18	123^2	140	27	3.1	7.9	109	47%	.314
2020	KCA	MLB	27	7	9	0	52	19	136	153	21	3.5	7.8	118	48%	.323

Comparables: Chase De Jong, Rob Whalen, Alberto Cabrera

A little glimpse inside the comment-writing process: At some point when you write a bunch of Kansas City Royals, you're going to get to a guy like López. The first thing you'll do is look at the pitch mix, check the velocity, see if anything shouts elbow injury. Then you'll go through the splits, looking for some ray of light, some potential building block or a better use of their talents. Once you have all that, you find some piece of media to serve as a metaphor, and you've got yourself a comment. Unfortunately with López, there's no split, no angle that looks better than the others: He struggled against lefties, righties, starting, relieving, home, away, every time through the order. It's all bad. We don't like to toss around comps like this lightly, but 2019 Jorge López was the James Fenimore Cooper of pitchers. At this point, if he can get the gopher problems under control, he might work his way up to Theodore Dreiser, but that's the limit to our optimism.

YEAR	TEAM	LVL	AGE	WHIP	ERA	DRA	WARP	MPH	FB%	WHF	CSP
2017	BLX	AA	24	1.25	4.25	4.47	0.7				
2017	MIL	MLB	24	2.50	4.50	9.45	-0.1	96.5	74.3	5.7	42.2
2018	CSP	AAA	25	1.50	5.65	4.22	0.3				
2018	OMA	AAA	25	1.00	4.00	5.79	-0.1				
2018	MIL	MLB	25	1.47	2.75	3.84	0.3	96.1	53.5	11.5	43.8
2018	KCA	MLB	25	1.47	6.35	5.08	0.0	95.8	50.8	7.4	51.1
2019	KCA	MLB	26	1.47	6.33	6.64	-1.3	96.3	54.3	9.5	47.3
2020	KCA	MLB	27	1.52	5.54	5.29	0.3	95.7	54.5	9.4	47

Jorge López, continued

Pitch Shape vs LHH

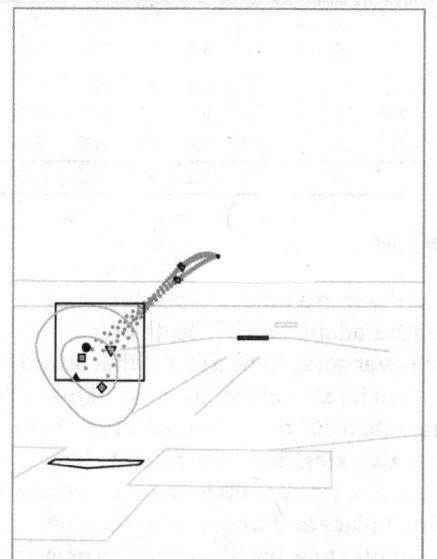

Pitch Shape vs RHH

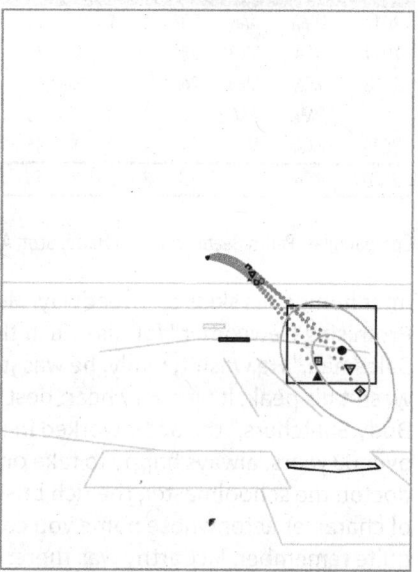

Type	Frequency	Velocity	H Movement	V Movement
● Fastball	28.4%	94.8 [107]	-7.8 [96]	-14.5 [104]
□ Sinker	26.0%	94.4 [109]	-13.6 [94]	-19.1 [104]
+ Cutter				
▲ Changeup	7.5%	87.9 [110]	-12.2 [95]	-26.5 [103]
× Splitter				
▽ Slider	7.9%	87.6 [113]	3 [92]	-30.4 [108]
◇ Curveball	30.3%	82.1 [112]	6.5 [96]	-45.7 [104]
⊕ Slow Curveball				
✳ Knuckleball				
▼ Screwball				

Kevin McCarthy RHP

Born: 02/22/92 Age: 28 Bats: R Throws: R
Height: 6'3" Weight: 215 Origin: Round 16, 2013 Draft (#474 overall)

YEAR	TEAM	LVL	AGE	W	L	SV	G	GS	IP	H	HR	BB/9	K/9	K	GB%	BABIP
2017	OMA	AAA	25	1	1	2	25	0	32	32	3	2.5	4.8	17	58%	.296
2017	KCA	MLB	25	1	0	0	33	0	45	50	4	2.6	5.4	27	55%	.303
2018	KCA	MLB	26	5	4	0	65	0	72	70	7	2.5	5.8	46	65%	.289
2019	OMA	AAA	27	0	0	3	13	0	16^2	19	0	2.7	8.1	15	64%	.380
2019	KCA	MLB	27	4	2	1	56	0	60^1	68	4	3.1	5.7	38	59%	.315
2020	KCA	MLB	28	3	3	2	54	0	57	65	7	3.0	6.3	40	58%	.313

Comparables: Pedro Beato, Donovan Hand, Scott Alexander

After honing his skills on Broadway, McCarthy won a Golden Globe for "Most Promising Newcomer" for his role in the 1952 adaptation of "Death of a Salesman." He wasn't, really; he was just never going to be a star. If that award wasn't his peak, it was very near: best known for starring in "Invasion of the Body Snatchers," the actor worked in more than 200 television shows and films over 60 years, always happy to take on the thankless task of the sheriff, the doctor, the schoolmaster, the rich businessman who got his in the end. The kind of character actor whose name you couldn't place and whose face you can't quite remember, McCarthy was there, no matter how bad the movie, to deliver the necessary exposition and keep the plot moving forward, because every movie has to end. This comment has been a metaphor.

YEAR	TEAM	LVL	AGE	WHIP	ERA	DRA	WARP	MPH	FB%	WHF	CSP
2017	OMA	AAA	25	1.28	3.09	4.29	0.4				
2017	KCA	MLB	25	1.40	3.20	5.36	-0.1	94.7	60.8	9.7	52.3
2018	KCA	MLB	26	1.25	3.25	4.46	0.4	93.9	67	10.1	49.4
2019	OMA	AAA	27	1.44	3.78	3.41	0.5				
2019	KCA	MLB	27	1.48	4.48	4.95	0.3	93.0	59.8	10.9	49.4
2020	KCA	MLB	28	1.46	4.98	4.85	0.2	93.1	63.1	10.4	50.4

Kevin McCarthy, continued

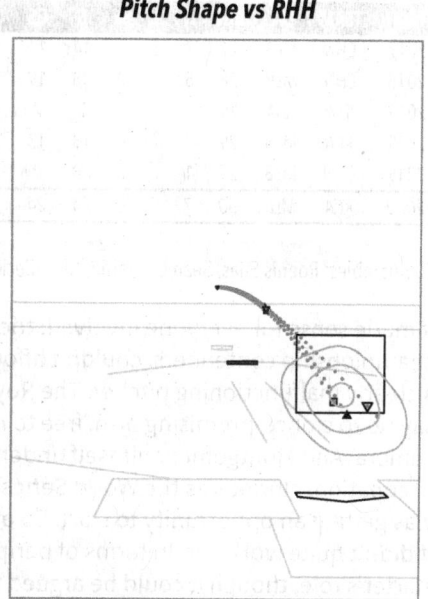

Pitch Shape vs LHH   **Pitch Shape vs RHH**

Type		Frequency	Velocity	H Movement	V Movement
●	Fastball	3.5%	92 [99]	-8.2 [94]	-17 [97]
□	Sinker	56.2%	91.5 [94]	-12.5 [101]	-24.7 [85]
+	Cutter				
▲	Changeup	21.8%	84.4 [97]	-13.2 [91]	-30.3 [91]
✕	Splitter				
▽	Slider	17.8%	86.8 [110]	0.8 [82]	-27.1 [117]
◇	Curveball				
⊕	Slow Curveball				
✱	Knuckleball				
▼	Screwball				

Mike Montgomery   LHP

Born: 07/01/89   Age: 30   Bats: L   Throws: L
Height: 6'5"   Weight: 215   Origin: Round 1, 2008 Draft (#36 overall)

YEAR	TEAM	LVL	AGE	W	L	SV	G	GS	IP	H	HR	BB/9	K/9	K	GB%	BABIP
2017	CHN	MLB	27	7	8	3	44	14	130^2	103	10	3.8	6.9	100	59%	.253
2018	CHN	MLB	28	5	6	0	38	19	124	131	10	2.8	6.2	86	53%	.309
2019	IOW	AAA	29	1	1	0	2	2	10	3	0	3.6	7.2	8	59%	.111
2019	KCA	MLB	29	2	7	0	13	13	64	78	12	3.0	7.2	51	52%	.346
2019	CHN	MLB	29	1	2	0	20	0	27	35	6	4.3	6.0	18	44%	.341
2020	KCA	MLB	30	7	9	0	24	24	124	138	15	3.8	7.2	99	52%	.319

Comparables: Roenis Elías, Sean Gilmartin, Brett Cecil

It made sense for everyone involved: the Cubs, fancying themselves championship contenders, couldn't afford to keep giving meaningful innings to a clearly malfunctioning pitcher. The Royals, at the price offered, could hardly say no to a once-promising arm, free to rehabilitate his trade value off (national) camera. And Montgomery himself understood the limitations of his current occupation, glorious as the World Series ring was, and that his best path forward was getting an opportunity to start. So all parties involved were pretty content. It didn't quite work out. In terms of peripherals, Montgomery improved in the starter's role, though it could be argued that regression did the bulk of the labor. The crafty lefty always had more of a starter's repertoire anyway, mixing four competent pitches, but the major change he made in his pitch mix heading south was to limit probably his best offering, the high-spin curveball that earned him a job in Chicago in the first place. Someone is contractually obligated to start baseball games for the 2020 Royals, so there's no harm in letting Montgomery see what he can do. (That last sentence was edited three times to supply the faintest praise measurable by science.)

YEAR	TEAM	LVL	AGE	WHIP	ERA	DRA	WARP	MPH	FB%	WHF	CSP
2017	CHN	MLB	27	1.21	3.38	4.31	1.6	94.5	53	8.9	44.6
2018	CHN	MLB	28	1.37	3.99	4.57	0.9	93.9	49.6	9.9	49.6
2019	IOW	AAA	29	0.70	2.70	1.69	0.5				
2019	KCA	MLB	29	1.55	4.64	7.16	-1.0	93.2	47.4	10	42.4
2019	CHN	MLB	29	1.78	5.67	8.83	-0.9	94.8	47.4	9.2	44.7
2020	KCA	MLB	30	1.53	5.26	5.00	0.8	93.2	49.6	9.5	45.5

Mike Montgomery, continued

Pitch Shape vs LHH

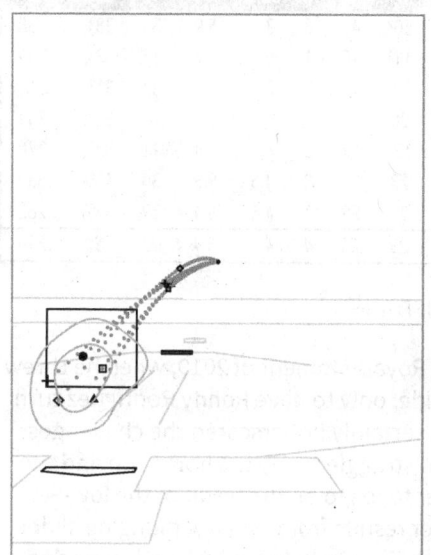

Pitch Shape vs RHH

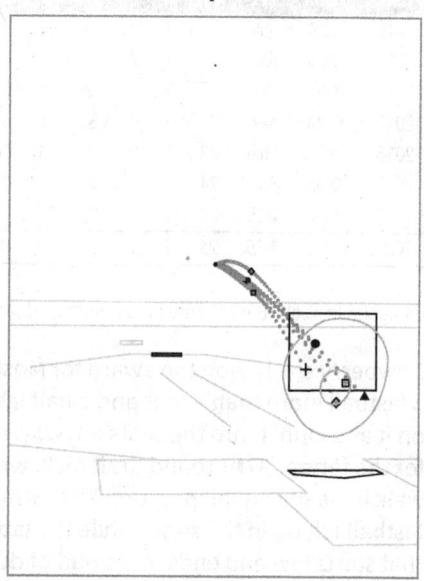

Type	Frequency	Velocity	H Movement	V Movement
● Fastball	15.3%	91.8 [98]	5.2 [107]	-18.1 [94]
☐ Sinker	26.9%	92.5 [100]	12.1 [104]	-19.2 [104]
+ Cutter	15.5%	87.6 [93]	-1.8 [100]	-25.8 [94]
▲ Changeup	21.2%	84.7 [98]	13.3 [90]	-27.8 [99]
✕ Splitter				
▽ Slider				
◇ Curveball	21.0%	77.9 [98]	-5.7 [93]	-47.6 [100]
✢ Slow Curveball				
✻ Knuckleball				
▼ Screwball				

Jake Newberry RHP

Born: 11/20/94 Age: 25 Bats: R Throws: R
Height: 6'2" Weight: 195 Origin: Round 37, 2012 Draft (#1123 overall)

YEAR	TEAM	LVL	AGE	W	L	SV	G	GS	IP	H	HR	BB/9	K/9	K	GB%	BABIP
2017	NWA	AA	22	4	2	15	36	0	50^2	45	3	3.4	5.9	33	38%	.268
2017	OMA	AAA	22	2	2	0	7	0	11^1	10	1	5.6	8.7	11	33%	.257
2018	NWA	AA	23	2	0	12	25	0	29^2	29	2	2.4	11.2	37	32%	.360
2018	OMA	AAA	23	3	0	3	16	0	20	13	1	2.7	7.2	16	51%	.231
2018	KCA	MLB	23	2	0	0	14	0	13^1	13	3	6.1	7.4	11	32%	.270
2019	OMA	AAA	24	2	2	0	22	0	28	29	3	4.5	9.6	30	41%	.333
2019	KCA	MLB	24	1	0	0	27	0	31	29	7	4.6	8.4	29	34%	.262
2020	KCA	MLB	25	1	1	0	22	0	23	23	4	4.1	8.4	22	36%	.296

Comparables: Jake Barrett, Fernando Romero, Eduardo Paredes

Newberry easily won the award for Most Royals Moment of 2019, when he threw a fastball more than a foot and a half inside, only to have Ronny Rodríguez turn on it and club it into the seats anyway. It certainly underscored the challenges for the former 37th-round draft pick, who struggled with the home run and the walk in nearly equal measure. The former tends to be the result of the low-90s fastball left up in the zone, while the latter results from a sharp, plunging slider that starts low and ends in a cloud of dust. Thanks to some luck with stranded runners, Newberry will likely get another shot to straighten things out, and if he can get that slider up and that fastball down, he might be able to tunnel his way out of that ugly DRA.

YEAR	TEAM	LVL	AGE	WHIP	ERA	DRA	WARP	MPH	FB%	WHF	CSP
2017	NWA	AA	22	1.26	2.13	3.55	0.8				
2017	OMA	AAA	22	1.50	4.76	4.73	0.1				
2018	NWA	AA	23	1.25	2.12	3.90	0.4				
2018	OMA	AAA	23	0.95	0.90	3.44	0.4				
2018	KCA	MLB	23	1.65	4.72	5.64	-0.1	95.7	54.8	10.3	47.1
2019	OMA	AAA	24	1.54	3.86	3.85	0.6				
2019	KCA	MLB	24	1.45	3.77	7.42	-0.7	95.7	53.2	12.5	42.6
2020	KCA	MLB	25	1.44	4.91	4.82	0.1	95.4	54.9	12.2	45.7

Jake Newberry, continued

Pitch Shape vs LHH

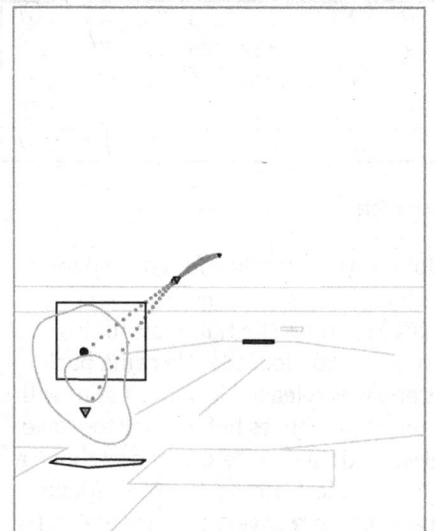

Pitch Shape vs RHH

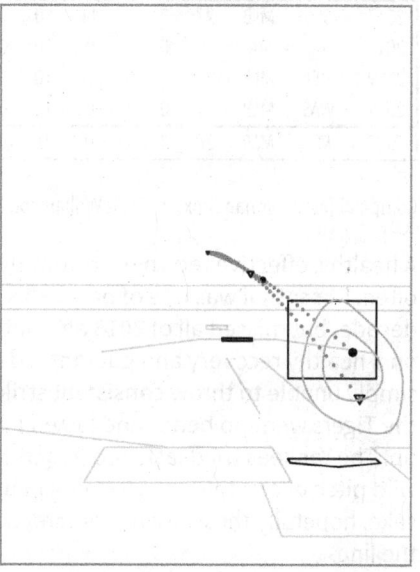

Type	Frequency	Velocity	H Movement	V Movement
● Fastball	52.3%	94.2 [105]	-3.7 [114]	-13.4 [107]
☐ Sinker				
+ Cutter				
▲ Changeup	3.3%	87.6 [108]	-5.3 [127]	-23.4 [112]
✕ Splitter				
▽ Slider	43.6%	84 [98]	5.1 [100]	-35.1 [94]
◇ Curveball				
⊕ Slow Curveball				
✳ Knuckleball				
▼ Screwball				

Trevor Rosenthal RHP

Born: 05/29/90 Age: 30 Bats: R Throws: R
Height: 6'2" Weight: 230 Origin: Round 21, 2009 Draft (#639 overall)

YEAR	TEAM	LVL	AGE	W	L	SV	G	GS	IP	H	HR	BB/9	K/9	K	GB%	BABIP
2017	SLN	MLB	27	3	4	11	50	0	47^2	37	3	3.8	14.3	76	40%	.337
2019	HAR	AA	29	0	1	0	10	0	9^1	9	2	6.8	10.6	11	50%	.292
2019	DET	MLB	29	0	0	0	10	0	9	3	0	11.0	12.0	12	56%	.167
2019	WAS	MLB	29	0	1	0	12	0	6^1	8	0	21.3	7.1	5	35%	.400
2020	KCA	MLB	30	1	1	0	16	0	17	15	2	6.7	10.7	21	43%	.297

Comparables: Jonathan Broxton, Scott Williamson, Keone Kela

A healthy, effective return from Tommy John surgery is taken for granted too often. Rosenthal was one of baseball's better relievers in the middle part of the decade, but missed all of 2018 after late-2017 surgery. The Nationals took a shot on a healthy recovery and guaranteed him $7 million for 2019. He came back simply unable to throw consistent strikes and was released in June. A stint with the Tigers went no better and lasted just ten appearances before they too gave up. The Yankees tried last, and Rosenthal walked three, hit a batter and threw a wild pitch over a third of an inning in his lone Triple-A outing. For Rosenthal's sake, hopefully these are merely steps in a troubled recovery and not the end of the line.

YEAR	TEAM	LVL	AGE	WHIP	ERA	DRA	WARP	MPH	FB%	WHF	CSP
2017	SLN	MLB	27	1.20	3.40	2.65	1.3	101.0	74.6	17.1	49
2019	HAR	AA	29	1.71	5.79	6.03	-0.2				
2019	DET	MLB	29	1.56	7.00	6.12	-0.1	99.9	68.8	12.2	42.1
2019	WAS	MLB	29	3.63	22.74	7.56	-0.2	100.3	75.5	9.5	43.6
2020	KCA	MLB	30	1.59	5.04	4.67	0.1	99.9	73.3	14.4	45

Trevor Rosenthal, continued

Pitch Shape vs LHH

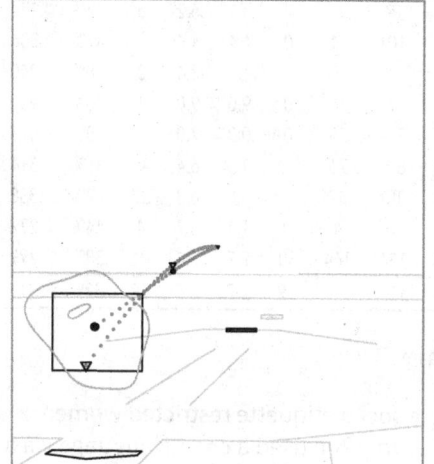

Pitch Shape vs RHH

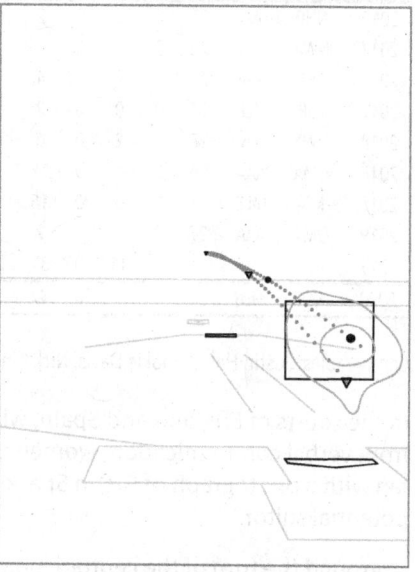

Type	Frequency	Velocity	H Movement	V Movement
● Fastball	72.1%	98.3 [117]	-5.8 [105]	-11.2 [112]
☐ Sinker				
+ Cutter				
▲ Changeup	3.2%	88.1 [110]	-9.6 [107]	-19.3 [124]
✕ Splitter				
▽ Slider	24.7%	88.3 [116]	4.6 [98]	-30.1 [109]
◇ Curveball				
⊕ Slow Curveball				
✳ Knuckleball				
▼ Screwball				

Royals Player Analysis - 73

Glenn Sparkman   RHP

Born: 05/11/92   Age: 28   Bats: R   Throws: R
Height: 6'2"   Weight: 210   Origin: Round 20, 2013 Draft (#594 overall)

YEAR	TEAM	LVL	AGE	W	L	SV	G	GS	IP	H	HR	BB/9	K/9	K	GB%	BABIP
2017	NHP	AA	25	1	1	0	2	2	8^2	6	2	3.1	6.2	6	52%	.174
2017	NWA	AA	25	0	0	0	3	2	10^1	11	0	4.4	4.4	5	47%	.306
2017	BUF	AAA	25	1	2	1	4	1	8	7	1	1.1	3.4	3	38%	.240
2017	TOR	MLB	25	0	0	0	2	0	1	9	0	9.0	9.0	1	20%	.900
2018	NWA	AA	26	3	2	0	6	6	33^2	35	0	0.3	7.0	26	45%	.321
2018	OMA	AAA	26	5	1	0	12	12	67^1	76	10	1.5	6.4	48	46%	.314
2018	KCA	MLB	26	0	3	0	15	3	38^1	47	3	3.5	6.3	27	47%	.338
2019	OMA	AAA	27	0	0	0	2	1	6^1	4	0	1.4	5.7	4	44%	.222
2019	KCA	MLB	27	4	11	0	31	23	136	164	30	2.7	5.4	81	38%	.299
2020	KCA	MLB	28	5	7	0	47	15	107	130	19	2.7	5.8	69	39%	.314

Comparables: Justin Haley, Rookie Davis, Nick Kingham

In the courts of England and Spain, where social etiquette restricted women from verbal communication, women of court often used a coded language via a fan with a photograph of Glenn Sparkman to demonstrate their disinterest in a potential suitor.

Around the turn of the century, photographs of Glenn Sparkman were posted in factory break rooms, until the government shut down the practice in an attempt to improve working conditions.

In Victorian times, children were often punished by having to draw pictures of Glenn Sparkman and then write their own name over the chest.

Wealthy Icelandic families suffering from poor harvests would often select a random peasant, name them Glenn Sparkman, then drive them into the sea in hopes that the evil spirits would be drawn away with them.

YEAR	TEAM	LVL	AGE	WHIP	ERA	DRA	WARP	MPH	FB%	WHF	CSP
2017	NHP	AA	25	1.04	3.12	4.20	0.1				
2017	NWA	AA	25	1.55	2.61	4.80	0.0				
2017	BUF	AAA	25	1.00	2.25	4.27	0.1				
2017	TOR	MLB	25	10.00	63.00	9.33	0.0	95.8	63.6	3.6	46.8
2018	NWA	AA	26	1.07	2.94	3.86	0.6				
2018	OMA	AAA	26	1.29	4.01	5.17	0.3				
2018	KCA	MLB	26	1.62	4.46	5.21	-0.1	96.0	56.6	10.6	48.9
2019	OMA	AAA	27	0.79	0.00	3.18	0.2				
2019	KCA	MLB	27	1.51	6.02	8.56	-4.2	95.9	60.9	8.2	49.2
2020	KCA	MLB	28	1.51	5.85	5.63	-0.2	95.3	60.5	8.6	48.8

Glenn Sparkman, continued

Pitch Shape vs LHH

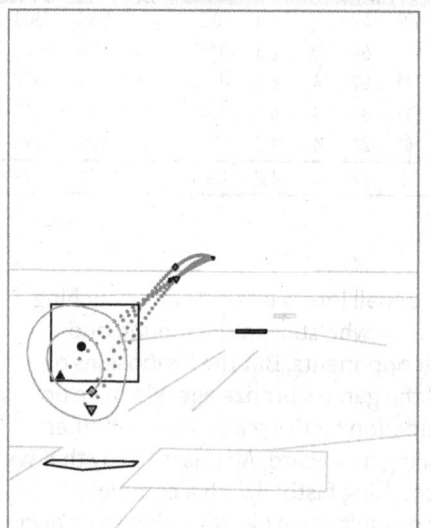

Pitch Shape vs RHH

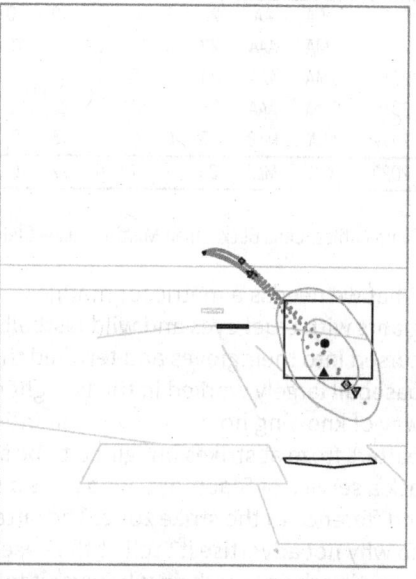

Type	Frequency	Velocity	H Movement	V Movement
● Fastball	60.9%	93.8 [104]	-8.8 [91]	-14.9 [103]
☐ Sinker				
✛ Cutter				
▲ Changeup	12.9%	86 [103]	-12.2 [95]	-23.1 [113]
✕ Splitter				
▽ Slider	6.8%	82.9 [94]	3.1 [92]	-35.4 [93]
◇ Curveball	19.4%	79.9 [104]	6.5 [96]	-47.5 [100]
✦ Slow Curveball				
✳ Knuckleball				
▼ Screwball				

Josh Staumont RHP

Born: 12/21/93 Age: 26 Bats: R Throws: R
Height: 6'3" Weight: 200 Origin: Round 2, 2015 Draft (#64 overall)

YEAR	TEAM	LVL	AGE	W	L	SV	G	GS	IP	H	HR	BB/9	K/9	K	GB%	BABIP
2017	NWA	AA	23	3	4	0	10	10	48^2	42	2	6.3	8.3	45	36%	.308
2017	OMA	AAA	23	3	8	0	16	15	76	64	14	7.5	11.0	93	41%	.279
2018	OMA	AAA	24	2	5	1	41	5	74^1	59	4	6.3	12.5	103	44%	.327
2019	OMA	AAA	25	1	5	2	32	12	51^1	31	4	6.5	13.0	74	50%	.262
2019	KCA	MLB	25	0	0	0	16	0	19^1	21	4	4.7	7.0	15	32%	.293
2020	KCA	MLB	26	1	1	0	22	0	23	29	5	6.2	8.3	21	39%	.349

Comparables: Chris Beck, Ethan Martin, Maikel Cleto

What we need is a metric for madness. Baseball lore is littered with slouching giants with cruel eyes and wild fastballs, men who stalked the mound and cursed into their gloves and terrified their opponents. But the Hraboskies of baseball largely worked in the twilight of the game's bronze age. We have no way of knowing how effective their intimidation tactics really were, whether batters froze at strikes imagined to be sailing headward. All this is to say that we ask a service of Staumont, who pairs a scorching fastball with a complete indifference to the strike zone. The latter doesn't seem like it's going to go away, so why not advertise it? Yell at the baseball, have arguments with spirits haunting the mound, do whatever it takes to strike fear into the hearts of mortals. Every little bit helps, and every little bit is probably going to be necessary.

YEAR	TEAM	LVL	AGE	WHIP	ERA	DRA	WARP	MPH	FB%	WHF	CSP
2017	NWA	AA	23	1.56	4.44	4.72	0.3				
2017	OMA	AAA	23	1.67	6.28	4.94	0.6				
2018	OMA	AAA	24	1.49	3.51	3.92	1.1				
2019	OMA	AAA	25	1.32	3.16	2.10	2.1				
2019	KCA	MLB	25	1.60	3.72	7.96	-0.5	98.3	69.6	9.2	46.8
2020	KCA	MLB	26	1.96	8.05	6.66	-0.4	97.9	70.9	9.4	47.6

Josh Staumont, continued

Pitch Shape vs LHH   Pitch Shape vs RHH

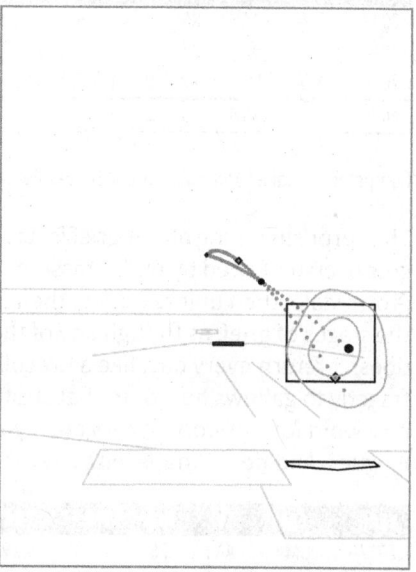

Type	Frequency	Velocity	H Movement	V Movement
● Fastball	69.6%	96.2 [111]	-1.1 [125]	-13 [108]
☐ Sinker				
+ Cutter				
▲ Changeup				
✕ Splitter				
▽ Slider				
◇ Curveball	30.4%	81.8 [111]	9.6 [109]	-48.6 [98]
✦ Slow Curveball				
✳ Knuckleball				
▼ Screwball				

Kyle Zimmer   RHP

Born: 09/13/91   Age: 28   Bats: R   Throws: R
Height: 6'3"   Weight: 225   Origin: Round 1, 2012 Draft (#5 overall)

YEAR	TEAM	LVL	AGE	W	L	SV	G	GS	IP	H	HR	BB/9	K/9	K	GB%	BABIP
2017	OMA	AAA	25	0	0	3	20	2	32^2	35	4	4.4	9.4	34	28%	.337
2019	OMA	AAA	27	2	4	1	37	12	54	46	6	5.5	8.7	52	46%	.276
2019	KCA	MLB	27	0	1	0	15	0	18^1	28	2	9.3	8.8	18	42%	.413
2020	KCA	MLB	28	2	2	0	33	0	34	32	4	4.8	8.5	33	41%	.286

Comparables: Jake Faria, Luis Santos, Brooks Pounders

The surprising thing about grief is its ridiculous longevity: eventually the pain gets overshadowed by embarrassment for still feeling that pain, long after it grows stale, then uninteresting, then actively dull. Then there are the lies about the stages of grief, as though any of them ever get completed, as if bargaining doesn't return every day, like a tax collector. Zimmer went from promise to tragedy to gallows humor to that strange brand of gallows antihumor, a password for the world weary and cynical. And then, finally, he made the major leagues. And now. What's left?

YEAR	TEAM	LVL	AGE	WHIP	ERA	DRA	WARP	MPH	FB%	WHF	CSP
2017	OMA	AAA	25	1.56	5.79	4.48	0.3				
2019	OMA	AAA	27	1.46	4.33	3.53	1.5				
2019	KCA	MLB	27	2.56	10.80	8.52	-0.6	98.4	60.9	11.9	47
2020	KCA	MLB	28	1.45	4.51	4.43	0.3	97.8	61.3	12	47.3

Kyle Zimmer, continued

Pitch Shape vs LHH

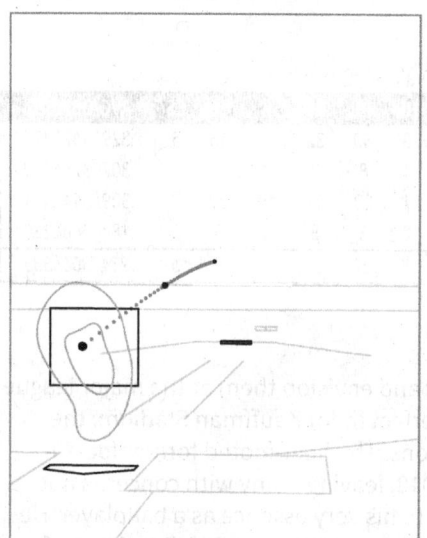

Pitch Shape vs RHH

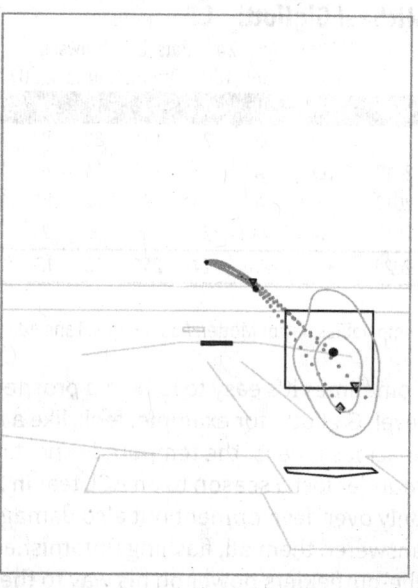

Type	Frequency	Velocity	H Movement	V Movement
● Fastball	60.9%	96.8 [113]	-0.5 [128]	-11.6 [111]
☐ Sinker				
+ Cutter				
▲ Changeup	4.8%	88.2 [111]	-4.9 [129]	-23.3 [112]
✕ Splitter				
▽ Slider	21.6%	85.6 [105]	3.1 [92]	-31.1 [106]
◇ Curveball	12.6%	82 [111]	4.1 [86]	-44.6 [106]
✪ Slow Curveball				
✱ Knuckleball				
▼ Screwball				

Kansas City Royals 2020

PLAYER COMMENTS WITHOUT GRAPHS

Michael Gigliotti CF
Born: 02/14/96 Age: 24 Bats: L Throws: L
Height: 6'1" Weight: 180 Origin: Round 4, 2017 Draft (#120 overall)

YEAR	TEAM	LVL	AGE	PA	R	2B	3B	HR	RBI	BB	K	SB	CS	AVG/OBP/SLG
2017	BNC	RK	21	191	30	8	3	3	30	32	21	15	5	.329/.442/.477
2017	LEX	A	21	100	14	5	1	1	8	8	20	7	5	.302/.378/.419
2019	LEX	A	23	279	42	19	1	1	23	27	49	29	7	.309/.394/.411
2019	WIL	A+	23	99	8	2	1	0	5	8	23	5	3	.184/.268/.230
2020	KCA	MLB	24	251	23	12	1	3	21	21	62	9	5	.234/.306/.333

Comparables: Taylor Motter, Adam Engel, Lane Adams

Sometimes it's easy to look at a prospect and envision them at the major league level. Gigliotti, for example, feels like a perfect fit for Kauffman Stadium: the spacious greens, the tempered expectations. The fleet-footed former fourth-rounder lost a season to an ACL tear in 2018, leaving many with concerns not only over development but also damage to his very essence as a ballplayer. He answered them all, flashing untarnished speed, defense and well-in-front-of-the-outfielders power on his way to the South Atlantic League All-Star Game. Then he went on to provide new ones after his midseason promotion. At his age and with his profile, there's exactly one type of major-league player Gigliotti could end up being, and it's not a given that he achieves it. But in the meantime, it's hard to blame Royals fans if they close their eyes and dream of a rangy center fielder who steals bases *and* takes walks.

YEAR	TEAM	LVL	AGE	PA	DRC+	VORP	BABIP	BRR	FRAA	WARP
2017	BNC	RK	21	191	168	27.2	.361	0.7	CF(39): -5.8	1.5
2017	LEX	A	21	100	131	6.3	.379	0.3	CF(18): 1.7	0.8
2019	LEX	A	23	279	148	27.8	.381	2.0	CF(59): 1.4	2.5
2019	WIL	A+	23	99	40	-2.5	.250	1.5	CF(16): -1.6, RF(6): 1.1	-0.2
2020	KCA	MLB	24	251	73	-0.5	.309	0.4	CF 1, RF 0	0.0

Kyle Isbel CF

Born: 03/03/97   Age: 23   Bats: L   Throws: R
Height: 5'11"   Weight: 183   Origin: Round 3, 2018 Draft (#94 overall)

YEAR	TEAM	LVL	AGE	PA	R	2B	3B	HR	RBI	BB	K	SB	CS	AVG/OBP/SLG
2018	IDA	RK	21	119	27	10	1	4	18	14	17	12	3	.381/.454/.610
2018	LEX	A	21	174	30	12	1	3	14	12	43	12	3	.289/.345/.434
2019	ROY	RK	22	27	9	2	0	2	7	2	5	3	1	.360/.407/.680
2019	WIL	A+	22	214	26	7	3	5	23	15	44	8	3	.216/.282/.361
2020	KCA	MLB	23	251	23	12	1	5	24	16	67	9	3	.222/.276/.348

Comparables: Andrew Toles, Alex Presley, Clete Thomas

Isbel is the platonic ideal of the fan favorite prospect: he does everything well, as defined by being slightly above average at every tool. He hits well for a center fielder, has a plus arm for someone out in left and demonstrates excellent range for a guy in front of the right field wall. Plus, he runs the bases pretty well for someone who might possibly get shifted down to second base. He plays hard, puts on a show at BP and generally throws out a stat line that entices one to scout. The last of these didn't quite work out in 2019, though even this can be explained away by emphasizing his hot start and solid AFL performance, and noting the broken hamate that ruined the span in between. This comment may seem like damning with faint praise, but it really isn't: Isbel is the kind of prospect you enjoy watching as he tries to put it together. He's also the kind who often magically transforms, five years later, into a forgettable fourth outfielder, the way we all wake up one morning to find we look like our parents.

YEAR	TEAM	LVL	AGE	PA	DRC+	VORP	BABIP	BRR	FRAA	WARP
2018	IDA	RK	21	119	195	18.0	.429	-0.8	CF(19): 4.5, RF(2): 1.1	1.6
2018	LEX	A	21	174	111	7.0	.377	2.8	CF(27): 0.8, LF(11): -0.5	1.0
2019	ROY	RK	22	27	155	5.4	.389	1.0	CF(6): 1.6	0.5
2019	WIL	A+	22	214	86	5.5	.253	1.8	CF(32): -2.3, RF(11): 0.5	0.2
2020	KCA	MLB	23	251	65	-2.8	.291	0.6	CF 0, RF 0	-0.2

Khalil Lee OF

Born: 06/26/98 Age: 22 Bats: L Throws: L
Height: 5'10" Weight: 170 Origin: Round 3, 2016 Draft (#103 overall)

YEAR	TEAM	LVL	AGE	PA	R	2B	3B	HR	RBI	BB	K	SB	CS	AVG/OBP/SLG
2017	LEX	A	19	532	71	24	6	17	61	65	171	20	18	.237/.344/.430
2018	WIL	A+	20	301	42	13	4	4	41	48	75	14	3	.270/.402/.406
2018	NWA	AA	20	118	15	5	0	2	10	11	28	2	2	.245/.330/.353
2019	NWA	AA	21	546	74	21	3	8	51	65	154	53	12	.264/.363/.372
2020	KCA	MLB	22	251	23	11	1	4	23	24	86	5	3	.220/.307/.336

Comparables: Clint Frazier, Byron Buxton, Jaff Decker

The phrase "Swiss Army Knife" might be the worst cliche when it comes to prospect writing, but Lee might also be the best example of them—because in reality, they only really work when you only have one or two tools out at a time. Every new season, seemingly every new look, the talented and amorphous outfielder looks like something different: one day demonstrating raw power, the next hitting everything on the ground, then looking awkward and sluggish in center, then carving up the basepaths. It's a little frustrating from a scouting perspective, but there are two important takeaways. One, regardless of which Lee shows up on a given team, they all average out to be pretty good, and two, there's always the chance that he figures out how to do everything at once. Even if he doesn't, and the 2019 version of Lee is actually his final form, it's one worth getting excited about.

YEAR	TEAM	LVL	AGE	PA	DRC+	VORP	BABIP	BRR	FRAA	WARP
2017	LEX	A	19	532	109	19.6	.338	-2.2	CF(67): -6.2, RF(52): 4.3	1.5
2018	WIL	A+	20	301	142	26.4	.371	2.2	CF(57): 3.8, RF(9): 0.3	2.8
2018	NWA	AA	20	118	81	1.2	.319	0.6	CF(17): 0.3, LF(9): 0.7	0.3
2019	NWA	AA	21	546	117	26.4	.374	3.7	RF(54): -6.0, CF(45): -5.7	1.2
2020	KCA	MLB	22	251	73	-0.5	.340	0.2	CF -3, RF -1	-0.4

Seuly Matias RF

Born: 09/04/98   Age: 21   Bats: R   Throws: R
Height: 6'3"   Weight: 198   Origin: International Free Agent, 2015

YEAR	TEAM	LVL	AGE	PA	R	2B	3B	HR	RBI	BB	K	SB	CS	AVG/OBP/SLG
2017	BNC	RK	18	246	27	13	3	7	36	16	72	2	1	.243/.297/.423
2018	LEX	A	19	376	62	13	1	31	63	24	131	6	0	.231/.303/.550
2019	WIL	A+	20	221	23	10	4	4	22	25	98	2	4	.148/.259/.307
2020	KCA	MLB	21	251	17	11	1	3	19	17	117	0	0	.156/.223/.258

Comparables: Miguel Sanó, Lewis Brinson, Tyler O'Neill

As bad as it looks, it was even worse. Matias hit four home runs in three games between April 13-15; from then on he shambled through a .118/.229/.203 slash line, trying to play through a broken hand that ultimately ended his season in mid-June. If there's any positive to spin here, it's that the excruciating pain of swinging the bat may have forced Matias to watch more pitches; for all the infinite Joey Gallo comps that have been made since his debut, he's never shown the selectivity of so many of his all-or-nothing colleagues. But even that's probably reading too much. The more prudent takeaway would be to dismiss the whole debacle as a lost year, and wait and see if the homers migrate back in the spring. And remember: always feel like you can tell people when you're hurting, whether it's your heart or your metacarpal.

YEAR	TEAM	LVL	AGE	PA	DRC+	VORP	BABIP	BRR	FRAA	WARP
2017	BNC	RK	18	246	84	7.4	.318	0.7	RF(52): 9.0	1.0
2018	LEX	A	19	376	97	18.8	.264	0.7	RF(75): -2.1	0.4
2019	WIL	A+	20	221	48	-4.5	.270	-0.6	RF(51): 5.6	-0.2
2020	KCA	MLB	21	251	28	-15.7	.295	-0.3	RF 1	-1.5

Kansas City Royals 2020

Brady McConnell SS
Born: 05/24/98   Age: 22   Bats: R   Throws: R
Height: 6'3"   Weight: 195   Origin: Round 2, 2019 Draft (#44 overall)

YEAR	TEAM	LVL	AGE	PA	R	2B	3B	HR	RBI	BB	K	SB	CS	AVG/OBP/SLG
2019	IDA	RK+	21	169	25	12	1	4	22	14	66	5	3	.211/.286/.382
2020	KCA	MLB	22	251	18	12	1	4	20	15	114	2	1	.176/.230/.278

Comparables: Brandon Hicks, Steve Tolleson, Jerry Sands

McConnell swings the bat the way one tries to kill a spider: a sharp, short slap followed by an almost instant recoil. The generically beautiful swings are languid, smooth, effortless, but there's something equally pleasing about his stapler gun trigger at the plate. Considered to be a first rounder out of high school, McConnell honored his commitment to Florida, suffered nerve damage in his hand, then rebounded in his senior year to become the Royals' second-round pick. He'll probably move off short before long, given that the team's best position player and best prospect stand in his way, which will make it vital that he unearth some plate discipline on one of those bus trips through the heartland.

YEAR	TEAM	LVL	AGE	PA	DRC+	VORP	BABIP	BRR	FRAA	WARP
2019	IDA	RK+	21	169	58	0.2	.341	0.5		0.0
2020	KCA	MLB	22	251	35	-13.2	.322	0.0		-1.4

MJ Melendez C

Born: 11/29/98   Age: 21   Bats: L   Throws: R
Height: 6'1"   Weight: 185   Origin: Round 2, 2017 Draft (#52 overall)

YEAR	TEAM	LVL	AGE	PA	R	2B	3B	HR	RBI	BB	K	SB	CS	AVG/OBP/SLG
2017	ROY	RK	18	198	25	8	3	4	30	26	60	4	2	.262/.374/.417
2018	LEX	A	19	472	52	26	9	19	73	43	143	4	6	.251/.322/.492
2019	WIL	A+	20	419	34	23	2	9	54	44	165	7	5	.163/.260/.311
2020	KCA	MLB	21	251	20	12	1	6	24	19	107	0	0	.175/.244/.312

Comparables: Austin Riley, Bobby Bradley, Lewis Brinson

It's been 18 years since a first- or second-round high school catcher panned out, in Brian McCann. (J.T. Realmuto was a third-rounder.) Melendez is targeted for an ETA of 2022, so by then it might be 20 years. Unlike many young backstops, assigned to the dish because of their general shape more than their fancy catching, the 20-year-old was comparatively lithe by the standards of his age. He's filled out in the intervening time, however, and FRAA so far rates him a talent, if hardly a prodigy. (Admittedly, there are limitations to all catching defensive metrics, especially on the minor-league side.) Meanwhile, his tendency to sell out for power in the batter's box appears to have suffered from a dip in the conversion rate. It's probably not as bad as it looks; Wilmington might be one of the toughest hitter's parks in the country, and he's only just now old enough to drink. Still, there's a lot of Zunino in the profile, and as underwhelming as that might sound to certain fanbases, a Zunino career would be a pretty fortunate outcome.

YEAR	TEAM	LVL	AGE	PA	DRC+	VORP	BABIP	BRR	FRAA	WARP
2017	ROY	RK	18	198	113	11.7	.385	0.1	C(30): 0.5	1.0
2018	LEX	A	19	472	103	24.5	.327	-1.7	C(73): 1.4	1.7
2019	WIL	A+	20	419	51	-2.7	.259	-0.9	C(71): 2.4	-0.4
2020	KCA	MLB	21	251	46	-9.8	.298	-0.3	C 0	-1.0

Kansas City Royals 2020

Salvador Perez C
Born: 05/10/90   Age: 30   Bats: R   Throws: R
Height: 6'4"   Weight: 240   Origin: International Free Agent, 2006

YEAR	TEAM	LVL	AGE	PA	R	2B	3B	HR	RBI	BB	K	SB	CS	AVG/OBP/SLG
2017	KCA	MLB	27	499	57	24	1	27	80	17	95	1	0	.268/.297/.495
2018	KCA	MLB	28	544	52	23	0	27	80	17	108	1	1	.235/.274/.439
2020	KCA	MLB	30	525	59	25	1	25	74	20	109	1	0	.245/.283/.449

Comparables: Terry Kennedy, Wilson Ramos, Joe Oliver

There are things we're supposed to be able to count on. Perez was given a day to recover from elbow soreness at the beginning of training camp in 2019, and then was given several hundred more after an MRI revealed

YEAR	TEAM	P. COUNT	FRM RUNS	BLK RUNS	THRW RUNS	TOT RUNS
2017	KCA	15629	-10.0	1.5	0.1	-8.4
2018	KCA	14052	-9.9	-0.6	0.8	-9.5
2020	KCA	22129	-9.0	0.4	1.2	-7.4

damage to his ulnar collateral ligament. Expectations are that he'll enter 2020 with fewer limitations and return to catching duties eventually, a relief for everyone in Kansas City who had to watch his understudies. (He will likely see time at first base and designated hitter, for some reason, while fully recovering.) When healthy, Perez is one of the most consistent performers in baseball, and it should be noted that for all the sabermetric shade cast upon him during the Royals' glory days, DRC+ appreciates his bat-to-ball and ball-beyond-fence skills more than other offensive metrics.

YEAR	TEAM	LVL	AGE	PA	DRC+	VORP	BABIP	BRR	FRAA	WARP
2017	KCA	MLB	27	499	112	19.7	.280	-1.3	C(115): -10.2	1.9
2018	KCA	MLB	28	544	104	9.1	.245	-3.7	C(96): -8.1, 1B(3): 0.0	1.3
2020	KCA	MLB	30	525	92	14.0	.267	-1.9	C -7, 1B 0	0.7

Blake Perkins   CF

Born: 09/10/96   Age: 23   Bats: B   Throws: R
Height: 5'11"   Weight: 181   Origin: Round 2, 2015 Draft (#69 overall)

YEAR	TEAM	LVL	AGE	PA	R	2B	3B	HR	RBI	BB	K	SB	CS	AVG/OBP/SLG
2017	HAG	A	20	572	105	27	4	8	48	72	118	31	8	.255/.354/.378
2018	POT	A+	21	305	39	11	0	1	21	42	67	12	5	.234/.344/.290
2018	WIL	A+	21	291	48	11	1	2	18	50	67	17	4	.240/.381/.322
2019	WIL	A+	22	352	43	11	4	6	22	52	79	18	7	.226/.345/.354
2019	NWA	AA	22	122	10	2	2	2	12	9	30	4	1	.218/.287/.327
2020	KCA	MLB	23	251	20	11	1	4	21	19	71	4	2	.200/.265/.303

Comparables: Aaron Hicks, Tommy Pham, Shawn O'Malley

The good news is that Perkins got his slugging percentage above his on-base percentage; the bad news is how. Double-A pitchers challenged the athletic center fielder with pitches in the zone, and suddenly his patience was no longer the carrying offensive tool it used to be. Sometimes, a low-effort swing just creates low-effort exit velocity. The hope was that a late conversion to switch hitting would offer just enough value to warrant the ninth spot in the order, or at least an inning or two of strong defensive replacement. Alas, unless baseball goes the football route and demands full specialization between offense and defense, Perkins' shot at the majors is looking grim.

YEAR	TEAM	LVL	AGE	PA	DRC+	VORP	BABIP	BRR	FRAA	WARP
2017	HAG	A	20	572	119	34.8	.318	7.4	CF(118): 8.4, LF(10): 0.9	4.7
2018	POT	A+	21	305	100	7.9	.307	2.7	CF(62): -6.6, LF(1): 0.1	0.6
2018	WIL	A+	21	291	101	11.3	.329	0.4	CF(61): 11.9, LF(1): -0.1	2.2
2019	WIL	A+	22	352	104	16.6	.286	0.2	CF(48): 4.1, RF(27): -3.7	1.1
2019	NWA	AA	22	122	62	-0.2	.278	-0.2	LF(15): -0.6, CF(12): 2.0	0.2
2020	KCA	MLB	23	251	53	-7.3	.272	0.1	CF 3, RF 0	-0.5

Kansas City Royals 2020

Nick Pratto 1B
Born: 10/06/98   Age: 21   Bats: L   Throws: L
Height: 6'1"   Weight: 195   Origin: Round 1, 2017 Draft (#14 overall)

YEAR	TEAM	LVL	AGE	PA	R	2B	3B	HR	RBI	BB	K	SB	CS	AVG/OBP/SLG
2017	ROY	RK	18	230	25	15	3	4	34	24	58	10	4	.247/.330/.414
2018	LEX	A	19	537	79	33	2	14	62	45	150	22	5	.280/.343/.443
2019	WIL	A+	20	472	48	21	1	9	46	49	164	17	7	.191/.278/.310
2020	KCA	MLB	21	251	21	13	1	5	24	18	98	4	1	.199/.259/.329

Comparables: Trevor Story, Cody Bellinger, Willy García

Everyone wants answers. You bought a book on the pretense that it would explain, in part, why Kansas City's best hitting prospect collapsed so badly last season. The Royals' organization would like to know why. Pratto himself would love to know more than anyone. And yet, sometimes there are no answers: There are no clues here, no brush strokes in the painting, no tea leaves, no magic eye puzzle. Pratto slumped early in the season, then slumped through the middle and ended on a slump. He lost his ability to hit for power and his ability to make contact. He probably got worse at Pop-A-Shot, too. In one interview he blamed the length of the grass for slowing down his hard-hit ground balls, and not the fact that he was hitting lots of ground balls. But what else could he say? This is how it is. Sometimes you work hard at something, and you do exactly what you're supposed to do and nothing happens. If you're really unlucky, they calculate the results to the third decimal point.

YEAR	TEAM	LVL	AGE	PA	DRC+	VORP	BABIP	BRR	FRAA	WARP
2017	ROY	RK	18	230	108	5.0	.319	-0.8	1B(51): 5.2	0.8
2018	LEX	A	19	537	111	14.4	.375	1.4	1B(125): -0.6	1.3
2019	WIL	A+	20	472	64	-7.1	.286	0.5	1B(122): 5.2	-0.5
2020	KCA	MLB	21	251	54	-6.7	.317	0.2	1B 2	-0.5

Bobby Witt Jr. SS

Born: 06/14/00 Age: 20 Bats: R Throws: R
Height: 6'1" Weight: 190 Origin: Round 1, 2019 Draft (#2 overall)

YEAR	TEAM	LVL	AGE	PA	R	2B	3B	HR	RBI	BB	K	SB	CS	AVG/OBP/SLG
2019	ROY	RK	19	180	30	2	5	1	27	13	35	9	1	.262/.317/.354
2020	KCA	MLB	20	251	19	10	1	3	20	16	72	2	1	.216/.270/.305

Comparables: Humberto Arteaga, Niko Goodrum, Leury García

Sometimes in the draft there's isn't a clear No. 1 draft pick; this year, there wasn't only one, but a clear number two as well. The son of 16-year veteran Bobby Witt, Witt the Younger's scouting profile begins with athleticism: He has the frame of a guy who's not quite too big to play shortstop, and he makes plays and throws with the elan of George Clooney playing Danny Ocean. Some scouts do worry that the contact skills will limit his total power, and that he'll never hit enough to be a true star; he does use the opposite field, but he was inconsistent during his showcase last summer. Still, given the legs and arm and glove, the floor appears to be solid regular, and that's some good floor.

YEAR	TEAM	LVL	AGE	PA	DRC+	VORP	BABIP	BRR	FRAA	WARP
2019	ROY	RK	19	180	94	4.2	.323	-0.1	SS(26): 3.3	0.8
2020	KCA	MLB	20	251	56	-6.3	.302	0.0	SS 1	-0.5

Jonathan Bowlan RHP

Born: 12/01/96 Age: 23 Bats: R Throws: R
Height: 6'6" Weight: 262 Origin: Round 2, 2018 Draft (#58 overall)

YEAR	TEAM	LVL	AGE	W	L	SV	G	GS	IP	H	HR	BB/9	K/9	K	GB%	BABIP
2018	IDA	RK	21	1	4	0	9	9	35	51	6	2.3	5.9	23	52%	.354
2019	LEX	A	22	6	2	1	13	11	69²	55	4	1.3	9.6	74	50%	.280
2019	WIL	A+	22	5	3	0	13	12	76¹	66	5	1.5	9.0	76	43%	.305
2020	KCA	MLB	23	2	2	0	33	0	35	35	6	3.3	7.7	30	43%	.289

Comparables: Cy Sneed, P.J. Walters, Rookie Davis

It's not impossible for the Royals to have built their entire 2022 starting rotation in the first two rounds of the 2018 draft. Singer, Lynch, Kowar and Bubic have garnered most of the attention from that promising class, but Bowlan recovered nicely from a rough pro start to follow along in their footsteps. The imposing right-hander out of Memphis remains the longshot of the group, mostly because his secondaries are the farthest away, but if he can find consistency, the Royals organization has shown they can make good material out of live arms. Perhaps most interesting is that so far, more than 20 percent of Bowlan's flyballs failed to leave the infield; either he's got some of that ol' Matt Cain magic in him, or there's a touch of regression coming his way as he climbs the ladder. Odds are still good that he ends up relieving, since those are almost always the odds. It's a fun story to root for, though.

YEAR	TEAM	LVL	AGE	WHIP	ERA	DRA	WARP	MPH	FB%	WHF	CSP
2018	IDA	RK	21	1.71	6.94	6.63	-0.2				
2019	LEX	A	22	0.93	3.36	3.60	1.3				
2019	WIL	A+	22	1.03	2.95	3.38	1.5				
2020	KCA	MLB	23	1.37	4.73	4.78	0.2				

Kris Bubic LHP

Born: 08/19/97   Age: 22   Bats: L   Throws: L
Height: 6'3"   Weight: 220   Origin: Round 1, 2018 Draft (#40 overall)

YEAR	TEAM	LVL	AGE	W	L	SV	G	GS	IP	H	HR	BB/9	K/9	K	GB%	BABIP
2018	IDA	RK	20	2	3	0	10	10	38	38	2	4.5	12.6	53	47%	.379
2019	LEX	A	21	4	1	0	9	9	47^2	27	3	2.8	14.2	75	49%	.270
2019	WIL	A+	21	7	4	0	17	17	101^2	76	3	2.4	9.7	110	43%	.286
2020	KCA	MLB	22	2	2	0	33	0	35	35	5	3.7	10.1	39	42%	.318

Comparables: Andrew Faulkner, Anthony Banda, Nestor Cortes Jr.

Well, that went fairly well. Most of the attention given to Bubic in his rookie season went to his delivery, with a windup like an exasperated sixth tug on a lawn mower, and the rather pedestrian fastball that emerged from the effort. The changeup was always going to be his best pitch, but it was the discovery of a second offering, in the form of a quality curveball, that forced opposing hitters back on their heels. There's still room for skepticism: It's not easy getting by in the majors without a decent fastball. But the wonderful thing about baseball is that no one needs to be able to do everything well, and if Bubic can continue hold his newfound velocity (91-94 mph) while throwing both breaking pitches for strikes, as he did in 2019, he should provide a welcome reinforcement for the initial pitching prospect sortie of Brady Singer and Jackson Kowar.

YEAR	TEAM	LVL	AGE	WHIP	ERA	DRA	WARP	MPH	FB%	WHF	CSP
2018	IDA	RK	20	1.50	4.03	4.28	0.7				
2019	LEX	A	21	0.88	2.08	2.40	1.6				
2019	WIL	A+	21	1.01	2.30	3.52	1.9				
2020	KCA	MLB	22	1.40	4.64	4.60	0.2				

Carlos Hernandez RHP

Born: 03/11/97 Age: 23 Bats: R Throws: R
Height: 6'4" Weight: 175 Origin: International Free Agent, 2016

YEAR	TEAM	LVL	AGE	W	L	SV	G	GS	IP	H	HR	BB/9	K/9	K	GB%	BABIP
2017	BNC	RK	20	1	4	0	12	11	62^1	64	6	3.9	9.0	62	44%	.322
2018	LEX	A	21	6	5	0	15	15	79^1	71	7	2.6	9.3	82	44%	.298
2019	ROY	RK	22	0	2	0	5	5	11	14	1	2.5	9.8	12	41%	.387
2019	BNC	RK+	22	0	0	0	3	3	10^2	11	1	10.1	11.0	13	33%	.345
2019	LEX	A	22	3	3	0	7	7	36	34	5	2.2	10.8	43	40%	.326
2020	KCA	MLB	23	2	2	0	33	0	35	37	6	3.9	8.4	33	39%	.308

Comparables: Scott Barlow, Seranthony Domínguez, Alec Mills

Ignore the ugly rookie-ball lines: Hernandez suffered a stress fracture in his rib cage before the season, and it took him half the year and some rookie-ball rehab to get back into playing shape. Signed out of Venezuela for a pittance at the autumn age of 19, the young man has expanded both his potential and mass over the past few years. While much of the latter has found its way to his midsection, the rest was channeled into his right arm, and he now sits in the mid-90s with his fastball. He's also equipped with a decent, if overly direct, slider and an inconsistent changeup as a third pitch. If you read that last sentence and thought, "Hey, that sounds like a reliever," well, congratulations. Hernandez is probably going to be a reliever, and he could end up a very good one. There's just enough time, as he avoids breaking bones and moving up the ranks, to roll the dice and find out if a third pitch magically reveals itself on the way.

YEAR	TEAM	LVL	AGE	WHIP	ERA	DRA	WARP	MPH	FB%	WHF	CSP
2017	BNC	RK	20	1.46	5.49	5.12	0.6				
2018	LEX	A	21	1.18	3.29	4.24	0.9				
2019	ROY	RK	22	1.55	7.36	2.90	0.4				
2019	BNC	RK+	22	2.16	9.28	6.11	0.0				
2019	LEX	A	22	1.19	3.50	4.19	0.4				
2020	KCA	MLB	23	1.49	5.31	5.22	0.0				

Jackson Kowar   RHP
Born: 10/04/96   Age: 23   Bats: R   Throws: R
Height: 6'5"   Weight: 180   Origin: Round 1C, 2018 Draft (#33 overall)

YEAR	TEAM	LVL	AGE	W	L	SV	G	GS	IP	H	HR	BB/9	K/9	K	GB%	BABIP
2018	LEX	A	21	0	1	0	9	9	26^1	19	2	4.1	7.5	22	59%	.239
2019	WIL	A+	22	5	3	0	13	13	74	68	4	2.7	8.0	66	46%	.305
2019	NWA	AA	22	2	7	0	13	13	74^1	73	8	2.5	9.4	78	46%	.323
2020	KCA	MLB	23	2	2	0	33	0	35	35	5	3.8	7.5	29	43%	.288

Comparables: Michael Ynoa, Esmil Rogers, Victor Alcántara

It's pretty impressive how we trick ourselves into enjoying mainstream movies. We sit down to a summer blockbuster, and enjoy a popular action hero play him or herself for the twentieth time while a different setting trembles and explodes behind them. And even though we know how it's going to end, how the hero is going to save the day, how they always save the day every single time because of some unforeseen and poorly signaled *deus ex machina*, we thrill as everything turns out okay. And then it wraps up, because of course it does, because it always does. The lava can be diverted. The salt does kill the aliens. And we leave the theater entertained, knowing that Kowar was fine all along, that he always going to have a good hard fastball with decent command, a rough curveball that'll go missing some nights, and he was always, always going to be a fourth starter. It never could have ended any other way.

YEAR	TEAM	LVL	AGE	WHIP	ERA	DRA	WARP	MPH	FB%	WHF	CSP
2018	LEX	A	21	1.18	3.42	3.71	0.5				
2019	WIL	A+	22	1.22	3.53	4.72	0.3				
2019	NWA	AA	22	1.26	3.51	4.67	0.3				
2020	KCA	MLB	23	1.43	4.93	4.92	0.1				

Daniel Lynch LHP

Born: 11/17/96   Age: 23   Bats: L   Throws: L
Height: 6'6"   Weight: 190   Origin: Round 1C, 2018 Draft (#34 overall)

YEAR	TEAM	LVL	AGE	W	L	SV	G	GS	IP	H	HR	BB/9	K/9	K	GB%	BABIP
2018	BNC	RK	21	0	0	0	3	3	11^1	9	0	1.6	11.1	14	59%	.310
2018	LEX	A	21	5	1	0	9	9	40	35	1	1.4	10.6	47	51%	.343
2019	ROY	RK	22	0	0	0	3	3	9	6	0	3.0	12.0	12	65%	.294
2019	BNC	RK+	22	1	0	0	2	2	9	13	1	3.0	7.0	7	59%	.429
2019	WIL	A+	22	5	2	0	15	15	78^1	76	4	2.6	8.8	77	49%	.324
2020	KCA	MLB	23	2	2	0	33	0	35	34	5	3.5	8.1	31	46%	.290

Comparables: Nick Maronde, Eric Skoglund, Taylor Rogers

After a fine season in High-A, Lynch made the Arizona Fall League his personal scouting showcase, wielding an awl-punch of a fastball that touched 99 mph. He also demonstrated an out-pitch-quality slider and a stern reminder of a changeup, both plenty good enough to classify him as starter material. Given that he's already building up enough mass to drop the "lanky" adjective, and the fact that he's shown that the velocity plays up in bursts, it's easy to envision a closer here if the whole starting pitching thing doesn't work out. That said, Lynch also lost two months to deal with a bum shoulder, and you're well aware of the cliché about pitching prospects.

YEAR	TEAM	LVL	AGE	WHIP	ERA	DRA	WARP	MPH	FB%	WHF	CSP
2018	BNC	RK	21	0.97	1.59	3.08	0.4				
2018	LEX	A	21	1.02	1.58	3.37	0.9				
2019	ROY	RK	22	1.00	1.00	2.09	0.4				
2019	BNC	RK+	22	1.78	4.00	8.31	-0.2				
2019	WIL	A+	22	1.26	3.10	4.47	0.5				
2020	KCA	MLB	23	1.35	4.32	4.42	0.3				

Brady Singer   RHP

Born: 08/04/96   Age: 23   Bats: R   Throws: R
Height: 6'5"   Weight: 210   Origin: Round 1, 2018 Draft (#18 overall)

YEAR	TEAM	LVL	AGE	W	L	SV	G	GS	IP	H	HR	BB/9	K/9	K	GB%	BABIP
2019	WIL	A+	22	5	2	0	10	10	57^2	51	1	2.0	8.3	53	56%	.325
2019	NWA	AA	22	7	3	0	16	16	90^2	86	8	2.6	8.4	85	51%	.301
2020	KCA	MLB	23	1	2	0	5	5	24	24	3	3.7	7.4	20	46%	.292

Comparables: Jeff Hoffman, Zach Stewart, Jon Gray

When a movie or a book gets reviewed, its score tends to be based not on its brilliancies but its lack of flaws. Brilliance in art, after all, is unquantifiable; mistakes can be counted. It's why every Marvel movie gets the same review score, and why Singer is a top prospect. He's exactly the opposite of what you don't want: despite a relatively low ceiling from a stuff standpoint, he demonstrates advanced command and has shown excellent durability. It's the kind of profile that makes one stand back and just admire the reliability, like a big truck sitting on the edge of a canyon in a Chevrolet commercial. If there's one concern, it's his lower arm slot, and what that might mean for pitching against lefties: He didn't exactly struggle with them in 2019, but the higher walk rate was evidence that he was worried enough to start nibbling. Still, Singer is as good a bet as any to be near the top of the leaderboards in innings pitched five years from now, steady, dependable, formulaic. It's not what you don't want.

YEAR	TEAM	LVL	AGE	WHIP	ERA	DRA	WARP	MPH	FB%	WHF	CSP
2019	WIL	A+	22	1.11	1.87	5.14	-0.1				
2019	NWA	AA	22	1.24	3.47	3.97	1.1				
2020	KCA	MLB	23	1.41	4.82	4.77	0.2				

Eric Skoglund LHP

Born: 10/26/92 Age: 27 Bats: L Throws: L
Height: 6'7" Weight: 210 Origin: Round 3, 2014 Draft (#92 overall)

YEAR	TEAM	LVL	AGE	W	L	SV	G	GS	IP	H	HR	BB/9	K/9	K	GB%	BABIP
2017	OMA	AAA	24	4	5	0	19	19	100^2	110	14	2.6	9.1	102	42%	.331
2017	KCA	MLB	24	1	2	0	7	5	18	30	2	6.0	7.0	14	39%	.431
2018	NWA	AA	25	0	0	0	2	2	9	12	1	2.0	4.0	4	41%	.333
2018	OMA	AAA	25	0	1	0	2	2	8^1	8	2	0.0	6.5	6	44%	.240
2018	KCA	MLB	25	1	6	0	14	13	70	66	12	2.4	6.3	49	44%	.261
2019	OMA	AAA	26	2	4	0	11	11	63	79	12	2.4	6.1	43	38%	.333
2019	KCA	MLB	26	0	3	0	6	4	21	30	5	3.9	1.7	4	36%	.305
2020	KCA	MLB	27	3	5	0	35	8	69	89	16	2.8	4.9	37	39%	.308

Comparables: Erick Fedde, Jason Wheeler, Cole Irvin

Skoglund lost half the season after testing positive for Ostarine and Ligandrol, and then lost the other half of the season by showing back up to work afterward. The lanky lefthander struggled to rediscover his rhythm in Triple-A, only to be battered around in September like a seal in a pod of orcas. Each of his pitches lost between one and three ticks, and no pitcher with as many innings had a higher contact rate than Skoglund's 89 percent. It's not like he was terrifying the worms, either; the balls were getting hit hard, and they were getting hit upwards. It's probably just best for everyone to pretend this never happened, hypnotize him into thinking it's still 2018, and starting him off in Triple-A to get ready for his second shot at the big leagues.

YEAR	TEAM	LVL	AGE	WHIP	ERA	DRA	WARP	MPH	FB%	WHF	CSP
2017	OMA	AAA	24	1.38	4.11	4.09	1.8				
2017	KCA	MLB	24	2.33	9.50	8.05	-0.5	94.4	63.3	7.1	54
2018	NWA	AA	25	1.56	4.00	5.44	0.0				
2018	OMA	AAA	25	0.96	4.32	4.18	0.1				
2018	KCA	MLB	25	1.21	5.14	6.20	-0.7	93.9	60.2	8	49.2
2019	OMA	AAA	26	1.52	6.14	5.86	0.5				
2019	KCA	MLB	26	1.86	9.00	9.80	-0.9	91.7	61.8	5.6	49.5
2020	KCA	MLB	27	1.60	6.92	6.41	-0.7	93.0	61.8	7.3	51.1

Daniel Tillo LHP

Born: 06/13/96 Age: 24 Bats: L Throws: L
Height: 6'5" Weight: 215 Origin: Round 3, 2017 Draft (#90 overall)

YEAR	TEAM	LVL	AGE	W	L	SV	G	GS	IP	H	HR	BB/9	K/9	K	GB%	BABIP
2017	BNC	RK	21	3	2	0	7	7	31	35	1	1.7	7.3	25	69%	.351
2018	LEX	A	22	1	1	0	7	7	41[1]	37	3	3.0	6.8	31	65%	.270
2018	WIL	A+	22	3	5	0	19	19	93	99	3	4.9	6.7	69	59%	.333
2019	WIL	A+	23	7	8	0	20	20	107[1]	95	5	3.6	5.4	64	64%	.265
2019	NWA	AA	23	1	1	0	9	3	23[1]	22	1	4.2	8.1	21	62%	.323
2020	KCA	MLB	24	2	2	0	33	0	35	34	5	4.0	5.1	20	48%	.262

Comparables: Drake Britton, Jason Wheeler, Josh Butler

Sometimes life is less about how well you do and more about how you manage people's expectations. That's what makes life interesting; by the time you're an adult, you have a pretty good handle on what you're good at, how you're going to deal with the people and the obstacles you run into. And then the world rolls some dice at you, and you have to figure out how to respond. Tillo got a particularly unlucky break when, after getting promoted to Double-A, he got invited to the Arizona Fall League, and because of the AFL's roster restrictions, he had to pretend to be a reliever for a few months. A lefty with a good fastball and wayward secondaries, Tillo was put in a predicament: perform poorly, and fall out of the team's plans, or perform well, and reinforce the team's choice to make him a reliever. He chose the latter, relying on lefty-righty splits to markedly improve his command. He'll likely get another shot at starting next year, but if he struggles early, the memory of his late-inning successes may get him typecast.

YEAR	TEAM	LVL	AGE	WHIP	ERA	DRA	WARP	MPH	FB%	WHF	CSP
2017	BNC	RK	21	1.32	3.48	5.06	0.3				
2018	LEX	A	22	1.23	4.35	4.12	0.5				
2018	WIL	A+	22	1.61	4.94	6.17	-0.9				
2019	WIL	A+	23	1.29	3.77	5.26	-0.3				
2019	NWA	AA	23	1.41	3.47	4.81	0.0				
2020	KCA	MLB	24	1.41	4.71	4.71	0.2				

Kansas City Royals 2020

LINEOUTS

Hitters

HITTER	POS	TEAM	LVL	AGE	PA	R	2B	3B	HR	RBI	BB	K	SB	CS	AVG/OBP/SLG	DRC+	WARP
Gabriel Cancel	2B	NWA	AA	22	513	70	30	0	18	69	34	144	15	2	.246/.308/.427	96	0.5
Nick Dini	C	OMA	AAA	25	213	34	11	0	13	36	21	29	7	2	.296/.370/.565	124	1.1
	C	KCA	MLB	25	64	11	3	0	2	6	4	18	0	0	.196/.270/.357	80	-0.1
Jeison Guzman	SS	LEX	A	20	490	51	23	5	7	48	25	98	15	13	.253/.296/.373	85	2.6
Nick Heath	OF	NWA	AA	25	375	55	10	7	6	27	39	116	50	9	.255/.332/.382	87	1.1
	OF	OMA	AAA	25	97	17	4	1	2	9	17	27	10	4	.256/.392/.410	100	0.4
Brewer Hicklen	OF	WIL	A+	23	494	70	13	7	14	51	55	140	39	14	.263/.363/.427	132	3.3
Ryan McBroom	1B	SWB	AAA	27	482	87	29	0	26	66	58	100	2	2	.315/.402/.574	141	2.6
	1B	KCA	MLB	27	83	8	5	0	0	6	7	25	0	0	.293/.361/.360	73	-0.3
Erick Mejia	2B	OMA	AAA	24	556	83	22	6	7	63	50	103	19	6	.271/.339/.382	75	1.6
	2B	KCA	MLB	24	27	3	1	0	0	4	4	7	0	0	.227/.333/.273	82	0.1
Emmanuel Rivera	3B	NWA	AA	23	534	59	18	2	7	57	25	77	6	2	.258/.297/.345	71	0.4

Gabriel Cancel moved up a level, and in so doing he became more Gabriel Cancel than ever before, enhancing both his strength and inaccuracy with the bat. At this rate he'll get to wear a major league uniform by 2021, and swing said bat a few times a week. ⓧ On September 15, **Nick Dini** accomplished something George Brett never did, when he doubled off Wade Miley. ⓧ **Jeison Guzman** isn't a name to remember yet, but put him down as a name to remember to remember. He's still fluid at short after having grown into his frame, and every once in a while, viewed in the right light, he looks like he can hit, too. ⓧ In any other chapter, a prospect like **Nick Heath** would probably go unmentioned, but Kansas City has a legacy of men like him, men who run with a blind fury and also hit with a blind fury, the emphasis slightly shifted. A toast, friends, to the Jarrod Dysons yet to come. ⓧ In the grand tradition of Ángel Pagán, Ranger Suárez and Rocky Gale, **Brewer Hicklen** hopes to translate his surfeit of raw athleticism into a spot on the wrong team's major-league roster. ⓧ The system works! The Yankees had no room for the Rule 5-eligible **Ryan McBroom**, so they sold him to a team with a little room. The Quad-A slugger got his shot, the Royals got to play the Luke Voit lottery for fairly cheap, and some meaningless September baseball became a little less meaningless, at least for the McBroom family. ⓧ **Erick Mejia** certainly is a baseball player. Capable of running and fielding, it's not impossible that he could develop into a utility infielder; it's also hard to imagine any team putting in the effort to find out. ⓧ The Royals had a surplus of international spending money, and they devoted a plurality of it to teenage outfielder **Erick Pena**, an athletic outfielder out of the Dominican Republic. Enjoy half a dozen years of Carlos Beltran comps, assuming everything goes well. ⓧ If you took all of the hitters in the Royals system and shoved their 2019 seasons into one man, you'd get **Emmanuel Rivera**, who took a step back with the bat and the eye in his first taste of Double-A. Or, he somehow instilled himself in all of them, and he's a villain who needs to be stopped.

Pitchers

PITCHER	TEAM	LVL	AGE	W	L	SV	G	GS	IP	H	HR	BB/9	K/9	K	GB%	WHIP	ERA	DRA	WARP
Scott Blewett	NWA	AA	23	1	3	0	5	5	25¹	21	2	2.8	12.1	34	42%	1.14	3.55	4.64	0.1
	OMA	AAA	23	5	8	0	18	16	81¹	115	24	5.1	6.2	56	38%	1.98	8.52	8.25	-1.2
Austin Cox	LEX	A	22	5	3	0	13	13	75¹	59	5	2.6	9.2	77	42%	1.08	2.75	3.86	1.2
	WIL	A+	22	3	3	0	11	10	55¹	53	6	2.6	8.5	52	34%	1.25	2.77	5.23	-0.2
Heath Fillmyer	OMA	AAA	25	2	3	0	19	10	49¹	48	8	4.7	9.3	51	42%	1.50	5.11	4.16	1.2
	KCA	MLB	25	0	2	0	12	3	22¹	28	6	4.8	6.0	15	42%	1.79	8.06	8.08	-0.6
Conner Greene	NWA	AA	24	3	9	1	21	16	97	101	11	3.5	7.9	85	46%	1.43	5.29	5.53	-0.7
	OMA	AAA	24	1	0	0	8	0	15¹	14	2	9.4	5.9	10	53%	1.96	4.11	7.46	-0.2
Foster Griffin	OMA	AAA	23	8	6	0	25	25	130²	134	20	4.4	7.6	111	50%	1.52	5.23	4.38	3.0
Zach Haake	LEX	A	22	4	6	0	18	18	75²	60	2	4.3	10.7	90	40%	1.27	2.85	4.28	0.8
Jesse Hahn	KCA	MLB	29	0	1	0	6	0	4²	7	1	11.6	13.5	7	43%	2.79	13.50	5.64	0.0
Arnaldo Hernandez	NWA	AA	23	2	2	0	4	4	23	21	2	4.3	7.8	20	35%	1.39	1.96	4.94	0.0
	OMA	AAA	23	4	8	0	22	20	105²	142	24	3.5	5.5	65	38%	1.73	6.39	7.24	-0.6
Alec Marsh	IDA	Rk+	21	0	1	0	13	13	33¹	30	5	1.1	10.3	38	46%	1.02	4.05	2.73	1.2
Wily Peralta	KCA	MLB	30	2	4	2	42	0	40¹	45	7	4.2	5.4	24	45%	1.59	5.80	7.94	-1.1
Randy Rosario	IOW	AAA	25	1	2	4	31	0	37²	46	5	3.3	7.4	31	61%	1.59	3.11	4.79	0.5
	KCA	MLB	25	1	0	0	6	0	3²	3	0	0.0	7.4	3	64%	0.82	0.00	1.91	0.1
	CHN	MLB	25	1	0	0	13	0	10²	12	2	4.2	8.4	10	59%	1.59	5.91	3.59	0.2
Gabe Speier	NWA	AA	24	1	1	5	17	0	22¹	20	2	3.6	11.3	28	41%	1.30	2.42	3.93	0.2
	OMA	AAA	24	0	4	1	30	0	40	41	10	3.8	10.1	45	35%	1.45	5.62	4.55	0.7
	KCA	MLB	24	0	0	0	9	0	7¹	5	2	7.4	12.3	10	29%	1.50	7.36	4.78	0.0
Drew Storen	NWA	AA	31	0	1	0	9	0	10¹	15	1	4.4	10.5	12	45%	1.94	7.84	7.05	-0.3
Stephen Woods	PCH	A+	24	9	3	0	18	12	86¹	71	2	3.4	8.2	79	54%	1.20	1.88	4.24	0.7
Michael Ynoa	OMA	AAA	27	1	1	2	17	0	21²	19	3	5.8	10.8	26	36%	1.52	4.57	3.51	0.6

Look, it's never easy pitching in the PCL, especially with the new rabbit ball, but **Scott Blewett** managed to make it look nearly impossible. It's time to abandon hopes for that third pitch and see if there are some sixth-inning appearances to squeeze out of that 6-foot-6 frame. ⓧ **Austin Cox** only earns a lineout this year, because despite his posting strong performances at two levels in 2019, it's hard to come up with 130 words explaining how. As a low-velo college lefty, the chance of a breakout is slim, but give him credit for developing his secondary pitches thus far. ⓧ Biceps, day-to-day: Five-seventeenths of a haiku, and an encapsulation of the entire 2019 season for **Yefri del Rosario**. Given that his age was his greatest virtue, it was a particularly harsh blow, as the young Dominican has plenty of work left to do. ⚾ As the great Will Rogers once said, "We can't all be heroes, because somebody has to throw them belt-high sliders when their bats go by." In that sense, **Heath Fillmyer** really is a hero too, in his own way. ⚾ If you're a team with a surfeit of roster spots and a long road ahead, you could do far worse than **Connor Greene**, a blunderbuss of a reliever in search of one weird trick. ⚾ **Foster Griffin** is not one of the Royals' fleet of wunderkinds, but at least he had the good sense to precede them. To survive in the majors, he'll have to limit walks and keep the ball on the ground, and he hasn't done both concurrently since Low-A. ⚾ Here's a reward for digging this deep in the lineouts: Former sixth-rounder **Zach Haake** has an inconsistent slider and a telegraphed changeup, but when he has them right, he has some of the best stuff in the system. The fastball has enough life and run to make him a bullpen asset at the very least. Keep an eye on him. ⚾ The **Jesse Hahn** that staggered back to the majors after a grueling two-year recovery was almost unrecognizable, abandoning his entire arsenal for a traditional fastball-slider pairing. Still, you have to wonder if he printed out curveballer Rich Hill's stats page, highlighted those lean 2012-2014 seasons, and maintains a little shred of hope. ⚾ With the most "can I see you in my office for a moment" energy possible, let us say: perhaps it's time to see what **Arnaldo Hernandez** can do in relief. ⚾ Third-round pick **Alec Marsh** has five average pitches and a low-90s fastball, which is the kind of profile that works as long as you never walk anyone ever. He passed the test in year one; next year will be the real proving ground, as well as the one after that, and the one after that. ⚾ **Wily Peralta** lost two ticks off his fastball, 10 percentage points off his strikeout rate and, ultimately, lost his roster spot. ⚾ The Cubs liked **Randy Rosario** enough to use him in a high-leverage spot in the 2018 Wild Card Game. A year later he was throwing low-leverage pitches for the Royals. ⚾ **Gabe Speier** has been included in trades for Rick Porcello, Cameron Maybin, Dansby Swanson and Jon Jay. Sadly, there will likely never be an annual comment about being traded for Gabe Speier. ⚾ After a failed comeback attempt, **Drew Storen's** life as Closer of the Future is formally at an end. But there are still so many Drew Storens left: Kiwanis Club Vice President of the Future, Country Music Singer of the Future, Mid-Tier YouTube Celebrity of the Future…. ⚾ Careful with the numbers here: **Stephen Woods Jr.** dominated A-ball, but he did it at age 24, thanks to a torn labrum that slowed down his progress. He'll have to prove that he can throw strikes against real hitters this year, but the stuff was worth a Rule 5 flyer for a team with plenty of bullpen room. ⚾ **Michael Ynoa** earned one last shot at the majors last offseason, and as with so many of his attempts, it missed the mark. This is probably the end of his career, or perhaps to put it better, the second end; the first one ended after nine innings, nine years ago.

Royals Prospects

The State of the System

The pitchers all took a step forward. The hitters all took a step back. Not the ideal Kansas City two-step.

The Top Ten

1

★ ★ ★ *2020 Top 101 Prospect* **#29** ★ ★ ★

Bobby Witt Jr. **SS** OFP: 70 ETA: 2022/23
Born: 06/14/00 Age: 20 Bats: R Throws: R Height: 6'1" Weight: 190
Origin: Round 1, 2019 Draft (#2 overall)

The Report: Some baseball families have more than just the job running through their bloodlines. The Bells all had roughly the same kind of offensive profile. You don't have to squint to see a bit of Mike Cameron in Daz's game. Vlad Jr. doesn't look like his father physically, but the swing is a dead ringer. Then you have Bobby Witt, who was a journeyman right-hander. His son and namesake? A potential five-tool shortstop. Witt has plus-plus athleticism and three potential 60-grade tools on the defensive side. His plus speed works whether ranging in the field or running the bases. The arm will play comfortably from deep in the 5.5 hole. And his actions, hands and instincts all portend a plus shortstop in the majors.

At the plate we can add a fourth plus tool: raw power. Witt has quick hands, quality bat speed and is strong enough to drive the ball over the fence when he gets extended. Well, only one tool to go: hit. And as usual, it's a tricky one for the prep bat. There's positive markers here. He'll show good barrel feel and the ability to adjust to pitches where they are thrown, but he also gets aggressive and you can beat him up with fastballs. His propensity to try to get long and drive the ball could make him vulnerable inside as well. An even average hit tool would allow most of the power to play and for Witt to be a perennial all-star, but if the profile ends up more like 4.50-tool, he'll just be a solid regular.

Variance: Extreme. Complex-league resume, the hit tool may play as fringe-or-below-average, limiting how much the power gets into games and blunting some of the upside.

Kansas City Royals 2020

Mark Barry's Fantasy Take: This dude is pretty far away, but there's a Trea Turner-y whiff with Witt's profile, albeit with slightly less speed and slightly more power. Does that make him another eponymous offspring like Fernando Tatis Jr.? Who's to say. What we can say is that Witt is already a top-30 or so dynasty prospect and could see time atop that list in the foreseeable future.

——— ★ ★ ★ *2020 Top 101 Prospect* **#64** ★ ★ ★ ———

2
Brady Singer   RHP   OFP: 60   ETA: 2020
Born: 08/04/96 Age: 23 Bats: R Throws: R Height: 6'5" Weight: 210
Origin: Round 1, 2018 Draft (#18 overall)

The Report: Let's make something really clear from the get-go: Singer is not ranked second in this system for his upside. He is a healthy, durable, consistent, strike-throwing, polished arm with an excellent performance track record and pedigree. He is a fiery competitor with advanced pitchability. Many pitchers boast some of these qualities, but Singer has pretty much all of them, and that is why he is here.

The fastball sits low-90s, up to 95 with run and sink, generating plenty of groundballs. His command of the pitch is plus, allowing it to play up past the average velocity readings. Singer's best secondary is a firm, low-80s slider that is above-average, but lacks elite movement, and is not consistently a swing and miss pitch. He is excellent at manipulating the shape of both the fastball and slider, allowing him to consistently give hitters different looks. There is a changeup as a third offering, but he rarely uses it, and it doesn't feature any kind of above-average action.

As I mentioned, Singer is theoretically everything you could want in a pitching prospect, minus the blemish of not really having a plus, swing-and-miss pitch.

That particular hole in his game was exposed a bit more in Double-A after he received a midseason promotion on the back of his dominance of the Carolina League. Some have qualms with Singer's mechanics, but to his credit, he still displays consistency and plus command, even with the whole inverted-W and low arm slot thing.

Variance: Medium. More reliever risk than you'd expect given his durability, but definitely a major league arm in some capacity.

Mark Barry's Fantasy Take: There's room for guys like Singer on fantasy rosters, but it's hard to imagine breaking the bank for a Tanner Roark-type or say, Jake Odorizzi pre-2019 strikeout surge. Singer should be a serviceable, back-end fantasy starter, which is certainly useful if not terribly exciting.

——— ★ ★ ★ *2020 Top 101 Prospect* **#93** ★ ★ ★ ———

3
Daniel Lynch   LHP   OFP: 60   ETA: 2021
Born: 11/17/96 Age: 23 Bats: L Throws: L Height: 6'6" Weight: 190
Origin: Round 1C, 2018 Draft (#34 overall)

The Report: Upon being drafted the general consensus was that Lynch was the weakest of the Royals day one selections; most outlets considered him a backend starter at best. Couple that with the history of arm troubles from Virginia draftees and there wasn't much room for optimism. Lynch forced a paradigm shift, and he did it in a hurry. His professional numbers have been impressive from the outset and his ERA has been better as a pro than it ever was in college. His strikeouts are down from his amateur days, but he's still a shade over one per inning and has upside beyond a mere backend arm.

Lynch is tall and lanky with a long torso and narrow frame throughout. He slings the ball to the plate and throws across his body a bit. He works mostly down in the zone with his fastball. In my looks Lynch worked up to 96 with the heater, but he's touched even higher. The fastball has life and is going to generate a lot of groundballs. His slider and changeup are both above-average pitches with the slider as the pitch with the most potential. It's inconsistent at present, but is an easy plus pitch when it's going well. Lynch will mix in a curveball occasionally, but it has shown to be a fairly lazy pitch in my looks. It's something he could use to steal a strike or two, but I don't see it as a legitimate part of his arsenal.

Lynch's mechanics aren't exactly ideal, and the history of arm troubles from Virginia alums is a legitimate thing to keep in mind, but that's a fairly short list of concerns. On the whole, he has a quality arsenal and has shown the ability to strike out professional hitters and get groudballs otherwise. If his command takes a step forward it's easy to see him as a staple of the Royals rotation as soon as the club is ready to start his clock.

Variance: Medium. Lynch has shown an advanced feel for pitching. He has three above-average pitches and there haven't been any hiccups as a professional. If he doesn't make it as a starter, he still stands to serve an important role in the bullpen.

Mark Barry's Fantasy Take: The lack of consistent secondaries screams reliever, in which case Lynch is definitely less interesting. I'm apprehensive in writing him off, however, as a huge velocity spike from college to the pros could portend other unforeseeable jumps in skills. Oh, and being a huge lefty also helps. I'll be monitoring Lynch early in 2020, but I'm not taking the plunge just yet.

───── ★ ★ ★ ★ *2020 Top 101 Prospect* **#96** ★ ★ ★ ─────

4 **Kris Bubic   RHP**   OFP: 55   ETA: 2021
Born: 08/19/97   Age: 22   Bats: L   Throws: L   Height: 6'3"   Weight: 220
Origin: Round 1, 2018 Draft (#40 overall)

Kansas City Royals 2020

The Report: A high pick who nonetheless surprised some with his breakout this year, Bubic showed a combo of stuff and pitchability that proved far too much for A-ball opposition. How well it plays at the upper levels and beyond is more of an open question though. I think he'll be able to get outs in the big leagues, thanks to an effective three-pitch arsenal and a good feel for attacking hitters.

Bubic sits low-90s with his fastball, touching as high as 94 with sink and run. There is sneaky swing and miss here, and he can also generate weak contact in multiple ways; grounders when he locates down and soft pop-ups when he saws someone off. The latter helps him neutralize righties and set up his secondaries. His low-to-mid 80s changeup is reputed to be plus-plus, and the fact that he struck out 11 on my look despite it being almost a non-factor on that particular night is encouraging, especially as regards to his curve. I really liked the pitch, especially the tighter version around 80 mph that plays as an out pitch with its late and sharp break. He'll also drop in a truer version in the low-to-mid 70s as a change of pace. Bubic has has a slightly unorthodox motion but is anchored by a strong lower half and generally repeats his delivery enough to command his pitches.

Variance: Medium. His arsenal is pretty well-established and he knows how to pitch, the margins are tight at the highest level and he'll need to be proficient and efficient with his curve and change.

Mark Barry's Fantasy Take: A personal favorite of mine, Bubic struck out almost literally everyone this season. Even though the K totals are gaudy, he hasn't really been tested by advanced hitters, so the lefty's ultimate upside is still TBD. For now, I'm viewing Bubic as a mid-rotation starter in real life or a fantasy SP4-5. He might not be elite, but he's easily better than a streamer and there's upside for more.

5. Jackson Kowar   RHP   OFP: 55   ETA: 2020/21
Born: 10/04/96   Age: 23   Bats: R   Throws: R   Height: 6'5"   Weight: 180
Origin: Round 1C, 2018 Draft (#33 overall)

The Report: All in all it was a productive year for the ex-Gator across two levels of the minors. Kowar's fastball ticked back up into the mid-90s, and despite less than ideal movement, it's an above-average pitch. His mid-80s change-up has plus projection, showing fade and dive and good velocity separation off the fastball. The curve remains on the fringy side, as it's a bit humpy and he can struggle to command it. Kowar has some effort in his mechanics and he be a bit stiff and upright, but he throws enough strikes and offers average command that could get to solid-average. It's not a sexy starting pitching profile, due to the lack of a breaking pitch—I wonder if a slider might work better here long term—but there's enough command and stuff that he should stick in a rotation.

Variance: Medium. Despite the plus velocity, Kowar would be a weird pen fit as a righty fastball/change guy, so he's going to have to make his way as a starter. Breaking ball development will determine how good a pitcher he ends up, even an average one could bump the projection to more of a true number three starter.

Mark Barry's Fantasy Take: Meh, I'm starting to gain an appreciation for the origins of Ben's deep disdain for back-end starters. Kowar looks like a back-end starter, is what I 'm saying.

6. Kyle Isbel   OF   OFP: 55   ETA: 2021
Born: 03/03/97   Age: 23   Bats: L   Throws: R   Height: 5'11"   Weight: 183
Origin: Round 3, 2018 Draft (#94 overall)

The Report: Isbel started off 2019 scorching hot, slashing .348/.423/.630 through this first 13 games before fracturing his hamate bone, putting him out until July. A hamate injury is pesky in that it takes much longer than just the rehab time to get that feel and confidence in your swing back. This probably explains some of his slumped July (.118/.132/.235) and August (.206/.287/.299). Isbel made up some of the lost reps in the AFL where he looked more like the early-season version. He was one of the best all-around hitters in the AFL and homered on the bigger stage of the Fall Stars Game.

Isbel displays good pitch recognition and discipline, which should allow him to continue to walk at healthy clips at higher levels. The swing has some length, and while there is some bat speed, it is by no means elite. Nonetheless, there is an excellent feel for hitting, and many signs point towards him being an above-average hitter at the big league level.

The best way to describe Isbel is that he is sneaky good at just about everything. He is an above-average athlete, with significant amateur experience in the infield. Although the swing isn't geared for home runs, there is enough strength to hit 10-15 per year. He is one of the best all-around prospects in this system.

Variance: Medium. Isbel's hit tool gives him a solid floor, but we didn't get to see him play a full season in 2019. If he ends up hitting for power, it's a versatile 20-20 contributor.

Mark Barry's Fantasy Take: Potential 20/20, you say? The speed alone makes Isbel interesting and rosterable in 200ish-prospect leagues, but if he stays healthy this season, and maintains his current level of production, he'll jump right into top-100 conversation.

7. Khalil Lee   OF   OFP: 55   ETA: 2021
Born: 06/26/98   Age: 22   Bats: L   Throws: L   Height: 5'10"   Weight: 170
Origin: Round 3, 2016 Draft (#103 overall)

The Report: It seems less and less likely that the power Lee flashed in the Appy League three years ago is going to find its way back into games at higher levels. The above-average raw remains, and Lee looks like he should hit for more pop, given the bat speed and good hips. But his approach often leaves him making less than ideal contact. His swing can get long and out of sync, and while he tracks breaking balls well enough, there can be too much swing-and-miss in the zone.

Lee has filled out a fair bit and is still a plus runner, although the speed can play down in center field as his instincts and routes make him more of an average glove up-the-middle. He feels like a guy where it could just click and he'd be a 20/40 center fielder that gets on base a bunch, but every year it doesn't happen, he looks more like a fourth outfielder.

Variance: High. Lee held his own as a 20/21-year-old in Double-A, but it feels like his hit tool is constantly walking a tightrope, and you are just waiting for it to take a plunge. It's an impressive collection of physical tools when he is going right though, and if Lee ever figures out how to get a bit more of his raw pop into games, he could be a plus regular.

Mark Barry's Fantasy Take: Life is what happens when you wait on the "If He Puts it All Together" guys, and I'm definitely guilty of holding on too long when the skills are tantalizing, like Lee's. For a guy who will ultimately be defined by the steals, the upticks in strikeouts and groundballs are troubling. Sure, he could put it all together, but I'd be taking the temperature on the trade market, hoping there's still some name value left to capitalize upon.

8   MJ Melendez   C   OFP: 55   ETA: 2023
Born: 11/29/98   Age: 21   Bats: L   Throws: R   Height: 6'1"   Weight: 185
Origin: Round 2, 2017 Draft (#52 overall)

The Report: The offensive output at Wilmington in 2019 was…not good. It was a throwaway season for Royals High-A bats, and Melendez was no exception. He was absolutely awful at the plate last year, and there is no way around that. The fact that every hitter in Wilmington struggled means something, but you can decide for yourself exactly what it means.

In 2017 the Royals paid overslot to pry Melendez away from Florida International University where father is the manager. The question with Melendez has always been the hit tool, and obviously his 2019 numbers didn't do anything to quell those concerns. If you disregard the hit tool Melendez looks like a star. He has plus raw power, a plus arm, and average speed—plus baserunning smarts and base stealing ability accompany it. He's more athletic than just about anyone behind the dish, he has soft hands, receives the ball well, and has a quick transfer to go with the plus arm. The problem is that the hit tool might be bad enough to prevent him from even getting over the low offensive bar for catchers.

He has significant timing issues. He really struggles to see the ball against lefties and takes more than his share of ugly swings. Melendez's ceiling is high, but there are serious concerns about his ability to get there.

Should Melendez continue to struggle at the dish, there's still a major league future behind it. His power and defensive abilities will be enough to land him a backup catcher role at worst. He's a likeable guy and handles the staff well. I hear nothing but good things about his leadership abilities. He's going to be the kind of player you want in your clubhouse even if he doesn't play every day. If the hit tool ends up a 4 or 5 then you have a player who could be a star. Unfortunately it has a long, long way to go.

Variance: Extreme. Again, it's all about the hit tool here. If he puts 2019 behind him and ends up with an average hit tool, the Royals have a star on their hands. If 2019 is a sign of things to come, Melendez is a backup catcher.

Mark Barry's Fantasy Take: "But catcher development is the nonlinear-iest of nonlinear developments," he said, hugging his knees while rocking back and forth in the corner. Fantasy catchers are bad, so the bar is pretty low, but a 40 percent strikeout rate and sub-.600 OPS at High-A is extremely not what you want. Until there are *any* hit-tool improvements, Melendez is off my radar.

9. Zach Haake   RHP   OFP: 55   ETA: 2021/22
Born: 10/08/96   Age: 23   Bats: R   Throws: R   Height: 6'4"   Weight: 186
Origin: Round 6, 2018 Draft (#182 overall)

The Report: Much like fellow 2018 draftee Daniel Lynch, Haake has put up much better numbers as a professional than as an amateur; however, he didn't have anywhere to go but up. Haake attended three colleges in three years and only put up respectable numbers at John A. Logan College (JUCO). His numbers at Arkansas State and Kentucky are not for the faint of heart. As a professional, Haake has managed a 2.55 ERA across 95.1 innings while striking out 108 batters. He wasn't originally mentioned in the same breath as the rest of the college arms the Royals drafted in 2018, but he has finally worked his way into the top ten alongside them.

Haake's fastball is his best offering. It shows plenty of arm side life, and he'll work it up to 97, although it sits more in the 94-95 range. His slider flashes plus, but it's a tease pitch. When he uncorks a good one it's tight and explosive, but he'll mix in more lazy and loopy offerings than you'd like to see. The change is an above-average pitch and his most consistent offspeed offering at present, and I've seen it make several good hitters look bad.

Haake is much rawer than you'd prefer an 23-year-old, ex-SEC arm to be. He shows poor posture on the mound and his stuff flattens out late in starts. His secondary offerings are near elite at times, but his fastball is the only consistent pitch at present. He has some mechanical issues to iron out on his developmental path, but he has a simple delivery and he already made major strides since being drafted.

Variance: High. He's a raw 23-year-old and there are things to clean up mechanically and with the secondary pitches, but if his development stalls he should be a safe bet to contribute in the bullpen.

Mark Barry's Fantasy Take: Whether due to injuries or an over-reliance on his heater, Haake sure sounds like a reliever to me. He could be useful in that role for onlies, but otherwise, not as much.

10 Erick Pena   OF   OFP: 55   ETA: 2025
Born: 02/20/03   Age: 17   Bats: L   Throws: R   Height: 6'3"   Weight: 180
Origin: International Free Agent, 2019

The Report: The Royals gave Pena the fourth-largest signing bonus of the 2019 IFA period, and he certainly looks the part of a potential five-tool center fielder. Often these (literal children) can look like the bat is swinging them as they try to max out for raw power because that's what gets paid. However, Pena's swing is already quite physical with good balance, bat speed and barrel control, and his frame could easily take 30-40 more pounds of good weight. The building blocks are all here, but it will be a while before we know if he sticks in center field or how much power he develops, or if he can actually hit professional pitching. It's hard to argue there isn't 3.8 million bucks worth of tools and projection here though.

Variance: Extreme. He was born the week Old School was released and has yet to take a professional at-bat.

Mark Barry's Fantasy Take: If you miss out on Jasson Dominguez, Pena might be a decent fallback. It's impossible to accurately project what the landscape will look like by the time this kid is ready (or really by the time this kid can legally buy lottery tickets), but I'd rather dream on someone like Pena than maybe six dudes on this list. If your roster depth can stand the wait, go for it.

The Next Ten

11 Carlos Hernandez   RHP
Born: 03/11/97   Age: 23   Bats: R   Throws: R   Height: 6'4"   Weight: 175
Origin: International Free Agent, 2016

Hernandez missed the first half of the season due to a stress fracture in his ribcage making it something of a lost year. He made 15 starts for Lexington in 2018 and finished 2019 again in Lexington having made seven starts for the Legends. He strikes out more than one batter per inning, and he does it with a fastball in the 95-97 range, an above-average low-80's slider, and a respectable change. Hernandez isn't very athletic, doesn't field his position well, and he's bad at holding runners on base. That said, he repeats his delivery surprisingly well and he holds his velocity deep into games. The warts are undeniable, but there is also a lot to like here. He signed out of Venezuela at the unheard of age of 19. His body has not developed well which is leading to some durability concerns, but he does a decent job throwing strikes and the raw stuff is good. If he can put together a string of healthy seasons and work on the body a bit, you'll see him creep up these lists.

12 Nick Pratto 1B
Born: 10/06/98   Age: 21   Bats: L   Throws: L   Height: 6'1"   Weight: 195
Origin: Round 1, 2017 Draft (#14 overall)

Just like the rest of the Wilmington crew, Pratto struggled at the dish. A full-season under the Mendoza line at High-A isn't what you want from your 20-year-old former first rounder—even in one of the worst parks in the minors to hit—but there were some positives as well. Despite his struggles with the bat, Pratto still managed to walk at a healthy clip (just over 10%), and four of his nine homers were hit in Wilmington, where power goes to die. He's a full two-and-a-half years younger than the Carolina league average. He managed 21 doubles despite his paltry batting average. Plus, he's still stealing plenty of bases (17) despite below-average speed. If I'd not mentioned his batting average in this blurb, it would sound like a respectable season. There is something in the water in Wilmington.

Pratto might not have the highest ceiling of the first base prospects you'll come across, but despite the down year, there is still plenty to like. He has big wrists and forearms and a strong build throughout. He's calm and controlled at the plate and he sees the ball incredibly well. He doesn't take many ugly swings. He may very well develop more power, and I don't think future 6 pop is out of the question. In the past I've said that I see Pratto as Eric Hosmer 2.0, but with quality baserunning ability, and I still stand by that sentiment. Don't write off Pratto just yet—he has the tools to figure things out as he develops.

13 Seuly Matias OF
Born: 09/04/98   Age: 21   Bats: R   Throws: R   Height: 6'3"   Weight: 198
Origin: International Free Agent, 2015

It has already been an odyssey with Matías and, at the risk of sounding trite, I must say that it is hard to believe that he is still only 21 years old. His first year stateside was 2017, with Burlington in the Appy League. He came in hyped and he struggled, showing only brief and rare glimpses of the promise that preceded him. The tools played in his 2018 Sally League campaign as he managed to crack over 30 homers in under 100 games, though he still continued to be plagued with approach issues and swing-and-miss tendencies. 2019 was a lost season, as he struggled horrifically in about two months of Carolina League action before going down with an injury in June. I saw him early this year and was blown away by both the potential positives and the ascendent negatives in his profile. Watching him take BP is a sight; his bat speed and natural strength produce easy plus-plus raw power to all fields, and when he makes contact it plays in game too. He's got a huge arm and plays a decent right field. Unfortunately none of this will matter if he doesn't start hitting the ball with more regularity. His swing often gets long and I saw him get tied up on fastballs in and go flailing at breaking balls down and away. His tendency toward a grooved swing is made even worse when his front foot starts bailing, and it all seems to have a tumbling effect on his confidence. The funny thing is that I actually don't think his underlying mechanics are all that bad; he has quiet hands, a soft load, and minimal stride. It might look bleak at the moment but there have been late bloomers with this sort of profile, and his alluring power potential should allow for one or two more fresh starts.

14 Kelvin Gutierrez 3B
Born: 08/28/94 Age: 25 Bats: R Throws: R Height: 6'3" Weight: 215
Origin: International Free Agent, 2013

Gutiérrez got a three-week cup of coffee early in the season, but otherwise had the Kelvin Gutiérrez season in Triple-A—decent batting average, not much pop. Even the Pacific Coast League and Triple-A baseballs couldn't coax much power out of his relatively flat, contact-oriented swing. While power comes later, the unspoken qualifier to that is "if it comes at all." That leaves Gutiérrez as a bit of a square peg on a modern major league roster. He's a very good defensive third baseman, but one that hasn't really played anywhere else. His physical strength and feel for contact means should be able to hit .270 or so—although he was overly aggressive and woefully ineffective against major league breaking stuff—but there just won't be much in the way of secondary skills or defensive flexibility. On the merit of his skill set he's a 45 OFP, a fringe regular. Gutiérrez is an averagish runner so he might be able to handle an outfield corner, and he'd probably be fine at first given more reps. We just don't know, and neither do the Royals. He's already 25 and more or less is what he is.

15 Brady McConnell SS
Born: 05/24/98 Age: 22 Bats: R Throws: R Height: 6'3" Weight: 195
Origin: Round 2, 2019 Draft (#44 overall)

McConnell does not look like your traditional second-round college shortstop. This is a class of prospects that tend to be around 6-foot and 180 pounds, good bat-to-ball, can run a little bit, more polish than projection, and might actually be second basemen. McConnell is listed at 6-foot-3, 195 lbs, and almost all that weight is in his lats, deltoids, and traps. He's broad, projectable and a premium athlete with above-average raw power. If he does have to move off shortstop, it will likely be to third, but he has a decent shot to stick. It's a first-round frame, and he performed well for the Gators his Junior year, hitting .332 with 15 bombs. The main issue with the profile—which was the case in college, but became more obvious in the Pioneer League where he posted a 39% K-rate—is that he doesn't have much of an approach at the plate. McConnell can be a pure guess hitter at times, and it's only going to get harder to guess right in the pros. This can improve with reps to a certain extent, but McConnell is also going to be more boom-or-bust than your traditional second-round college shortstop.

16 Wilmin Candelario   SS
Born: 09/11/01   Age: 18   Bats: B   Throws: R   Height: 5'11"   Weight: 165
Origin: International Free Agent, 2018

Candelario signed for 850k out of the Dominican in 2018. Most of your six-figure IFAs are going to be signed as shortstops or center fielders, no matter how likely or unlikely it is they stick up the middle as they proceed up the organizational ladder (or even by the time they head stateside). Candelario is a shortstop. That's not going to be an issue. He's a potential plus one as well, with about the smoothest hands and actions you will see. He lacks physicality at present, so he will need to add strength to avoid having the bat knocked out of his hands against better velocity. It's not a frame that's likely to add that much bulk though, which is both good and bad. He should keep the quick-twitch athleticism you need at the 6, but he is unlikely to make the kind of hard contact with lift to be much of a power threat. Then again, projecting a 17-year-old's physical development with any sort of confidence is more soothsay than science.

17 Austin Cox   LHP
Born: 03/28/97   Age: 23   Bats: L   Throws: L   Height: 6'4"   Weight: 185
Origin: Round 5, 2018 Draft (#152 overall)

Cox is a fifth-rounder out of a small college, who I like more than some similar profiles with bigger names. He's a six-foot-four lefty with a solid pitcher's frame, although he's pretty well filled out and doesn't offer much in the way of projection. The fastball sits either side of 90, but he can hit 94 when he needs it. He commands the heater pretty well, especially glove-side where he uses it to get ahead against righties. He throws what looked to me like three distinct and viable breaking balls, all of which work to neutralize the platoon advantage. The strongest of them is a sharp power curve around 80 mph that flashed plus for me, with its late 1-7 action. Cox also likes to mix in a hard slider around 83-86 with almost cutter-like movement and a mid-70s 12-6 curve. These three offerings could all be lumped into an omnibus "breaking ball" category if you like, but each serves in its own purpose. The mid-80s change looked decent as well, with some split action to it. The stuff might be a bit short as he advances, but he's done well with it thus far.

18 Alec Marsh   RHP
Born: 05/14/98   Age: 22   Bats: R   Throws: R   Height: 6'2"   Weight: 220
Origin: Round 2, 2019 Draft (#70 overall)

Kansas City Royals 2020

Marsh on the other hand is very much your traditional second-round college pick. He's a sturdy lad who lacks much in the way of future projection and will throw four pitches for strikes, all within a half grade or so of average. He works primarily off a low-90s fastball which will flash decent sink from his high-three-quarters slot. There's two breaking balls, a slider and a curve that can smush together a bit around 80 mph, but tease out more distinctively in the mid-70s or low-80s. Both have average potential, but are more likely to end up fringy. The change is a bit crude as he has to really work to turn it over at present. Marsh has a chance to be a backend starter if he can refine the secondaries, but may lack a bat-missing option at higher levels and settle in more as a swingman or middle relief option.

19 Grant Gambrell   RHP
Born: 11/21/97   Age: 22   Bats: L   Throws: R   Height: 6'4"   Weight: 225
Origin: Round 3, 2019 Draft (#80 overall)

Gambrell was taken ten spots after Marsh in the 2019 draft and that might overstate the gap between them as pitching prospects. Gambrell is a bit taller, but just as sturdy of frame. He will show a little more velocity at times, getting up to 95 occasionally, but his fastball was inconsistent across his junior year at Oregon State and first pro summer. His secondaries are a bit less advanced than Marsh as well, although he flashed a potentially average slider in the pros. There's some feel for the change, but it's inconsistent. Gambrell has a chance to be a backend starter if he can refine the secondaries, but may lack a bat-missing option at higher levels and settle in more as a swingman or middle relief option.

20 Richard Lovelady   LHP
Born: 07/07/95   Age: 24   Bats: L   Throws: L   Height: 6'0"   Weight: 175
Origin: Round 10, 2016 Draft (#313 overall)

Lovelady is a 95-and-a-slider guy, but he's a lefty 95-and-a-slider guy. The stuff got worn out a bit in his first outings in las grandes ligas, as the low slot and long arm action give righties an awfully long look at the baseball, and the slider doesn't always have ideal depth to cross over. This was his first real performance blip, and several of your favorite advanced metrics suggest he was maybe a tad unlucky. There's always going to be thin margins and potential platoon issues for Lovelady, but he should get plenty more shots at a meaningful bullpen role since he's a lefty 95-and-a-slider guy.

Personal Cheeseball

PC Michael Gigliotti   OF
Born: 02/14/96   Age: 24   Bats: L   Throws: L   Height: 6'1"   Weight: 180
Origin: Round 4, 2017 Draft (#120 overall)

Gigliotti has been hanging around these lists for a long time for someone who has yet to accrue 100 at-bats above Low-A. He was really looking to hit his stride at the outset of the 2018 season, but a knee injury six games into the year put an end to that campaign. Gigliotti will be 24 when the 2020 season begins. As with the rest of the Blue Rocks he'll be happy to put 2019 in the rearview. All told, as a professional he is slashing a very respectable .296/.392/.407. The hit tool, speed, and glove are going to be the tools to make or break him. He is short to the ball with a flat, handsy swing, and he's one of the few players in baseball still looking to keep the ball out of the air. Only once has he hit more than one home run as a professional. He's speedy—near plus-plus—and can be expected to tame centerfield at Kauffman should he get there, as the glove won't be the question. If the hit tool doesn't do the trick, Gigliotti may not make it to Kansas City.

Low Minors Sleeper

LMS

Brewer Hicklen   OF
Born: 02/09/96   Age: 24   Bats: R   Throws: R   Height: 6'2"   Weight: 208
Origin: Round 7, 2017 Draft (#210 overall)

Hicklen is an athletic guy who shows an impressive combination of plus speed and plus raw power. He committed to UAB out of high school to play both football and baseball, and he looks exactly as you'd expect a two-way commit to look, checking in at 6-foot-2 and 208-pounds. Hicklen was virtually the only Wilmington bat to put up respectable numbers last year when he slashed .263/.363/.427 while stealing an impressive 39 bags. He's a three true outcomes sort of player with a 9.2 percent walk rate and 28 percent k-rate as a professional. He'll make some really impressive plays in the outfield, but will sometimes make routine plays more challenging than they are. He has solid bat speed, but it's mostly strength-based power. He will be 24 when the 2020 season begins, and will likely be given his first crack at upper minors competition. Swing-and-miss will be the big limiting factor for Hicklen, and his 26 K's in 47 at-bats in the 2019 AFL didn't do anything to calm those concerns. Cutting down on the whiffs should be his main concern moving forward.

Top Talents 25 and Under (as of 4/1/2020)

1. Adalberto Mondesi
2. Bobby Witt Jr.
3. Brady Singer
4. Daniel Lynch
5. Kris Bubic
6. Jackson Kowar
7. Brad Keller

Kansas City Royals 2020

8. Kyle Isbel
9. Khalil Lee
10. Nicky Lopez

This is probably what a 25U list should look like for a rebuilding club: Light on big league talent while tilting heavily toward potential on the farm.

Adalberto Mondesi has been a mainstay on this list since 2013. 2013! He debuted at number six that year and, as the World Championship generation graduated off this list, moved his way to the top. It's a perch he's occupied for three consecutive seasons. And with good reason. He's an impact player with the glove and the wheels, along with plenty of potential in the bat. However, Mondesi took a step back with a 75 DRC+ in 2019 in a season that saw his power regress and his OBP dip below .300. The Royals were aggressive with his movement through the system, but even with the offensive struggles he finally feels at home at the 6 at Kauffman Stadium. Another lingering question is his durability. He played just 102 games last season and ended the year on the IL.

Following last summer's number one pick and the Class of 2018 college arms is Keller, a former Rule 5 selection from the Diamondbacks organization. (That kind of says something about the state of the Royals, doesn't it?) Keller generates a ground ball on nearly half the balls put in play against him, which in the age of defensive shifts is a very good thing. Keller also doesn't miss many bats and his 6.6 K/9 was the sixth lowest strikeout rate among qualified starters. He's been the Royals' best starter in each of the last two seasons but should slide his way further back in the rotation as the young arms ahead of him on this list arrive in Kansas City.

Lopez saw a steady diet of inside fastballs in his major league debut and struggled to adjust. A wrist injury didn't help the cause, but neither did an approach that yielded a 4.5 percent walk rate. At every stop along the way to The Show, Lopez has routinely walked in over 10 percent of his plate appearances. He's spent the winter bulking up to help the former issue. Time will tell how he will handle the latter.

It's not an especially optimistic assessment of the major league talent on this U25 list, but that's not the really aim for a rebuilding club. The future, the Royals hope, is in the development of their pitching prospects.

Part 3: Featured Articles

The Baseball Is Juiced (Again)

Robert Arthur

This article originally appeared at Baseball Prospectus on April 5, 2019.

It started when the normally reliable Chris Sale got lit up for three homers by the Mariners in the Red Sox's season opener. It was part of a record number of taters that flew on Opening Day, as starters from Sale to Zack Greinke were taken deep by the handful. Then Christian Yelich hit a home run in each of his first four games, tying yet another MLB record, this one for consecutive games with a dinger to start a season.

It didn't take long for fans and players to begin whispering and tweeting about the baseballs being juiced again. It's early yet for us to come to any definitive conclusion about the 2019 season, but preliminary data shows that the baseball has returned to its aerodynamic peak. Whether that means this season will smash home run records like 2017 did remains to be seen.

Before home run explosion over the last few years, no one worried too much about the baseball's air resistance. While MLB and Rawlings (the company that manufactures the official baseballs) kept track of dozens of metrics to make sure that the ball was consistent from month to month, they didn't measure drag.

But drag is incredibly important in determining how likely a hitter is to knock one out of the park. As baseballs become more aerodynamic, they travel further given a certain initial velocity. A deep fly ball that might have been caught at the warning track can instead go into the first row of the stands. A three percent change in drag coefficient can work to add about five feet to a well-hit fly ball, which can in turn increase home runs league wide by an astounding 10-15 percent.

It's possible to measure the aerodynamics of the baseball using the pitch-tracking radars currently in place in each MLB ballpark. By calculating the loss of speed from when the pitch is released to when it crosses the plate, you can directly measure the drag coefficient on the baseball. I first wrote about the role of decreasing drag in boosting home runs in 2017, and MLB's commission of scientists and statisticians later confirmed that the more aerodynamic baseballs in use that year were largely to blame for the spike in home runs. The same commission rejected some alternate hypotheses, like rising temperatures and a league-wide boost in launch angle pushing more balls over the fence.

The current era has featured some large fluctuations in drag coefficient, leading to first an explosion in 2016 and 2017, and then a dialing back of homers last year. Curious about the record-breaking home run tallies in the last few days, I used the same methodology to measure the aerodynamics of the baseballs so far in 2019.

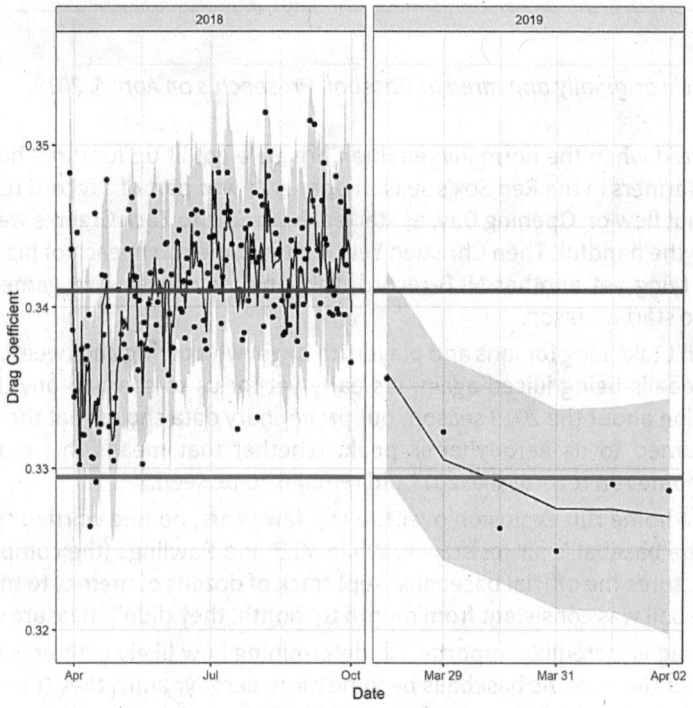

We're only a week into the 2019 season, but the drag numbers so far are among the lowest recorded in the last calendar year. With apologies for gory math, the current 2019 season average drag coefficient (the red line) would be below the 95 percent credible interval (the shaded area) for about nine-tenths of the 2018 season. (I used a Bayesian Random Walk model implemented in INLA to calculate these credible intervals, averaging the drag numbers in each game and adjusting for park.)

There were only a handful of six-day stretches in 2018 that had drag numbers below what we're seeing now, and most were in late June and early July. All of this means that 2019's data so far is quite a bit different than what we saw through most of last year.

These drag coefficients factor out the effects of temperature and air density, so they aren't a product of April cold. However, the numbers could be deceptive if the radars used to track pitches have changed from year to year. I consulted with some experts within baseball who were not aware of any specific modifications to the radar this year that could produce this pattern, but it's an important caveat of which to be aware.

On the one hand, it's only been six days, and we don't quite have the statistical basis to say that these drag coefficients are unprecedented compared to 2018. On the other hand, we've witnessed about 5,000 fastballs so far this season, so it's not as if our sample size is small. At least so far, the baseball has played like it's much more aerodynamic than it was last year. In fact, the current drag coefficient is really only comparable to 2017, when the baseballs were more aerodynamic than they had been in at least a decade.

It's not just fancy radar tracking indicating that the baseball is flying through the air more easily. The current number of home runs per game (as of this writing) is the highest it's been since the heady days of 2017, the year that teams and players broke dinger-related records everywhere you looked. That's especially remarkable considering that we're in what is typically the coldest part of the regular season, when lower temperatures and higher winds tend to suppress offense and keep balls in the air within the park. Comparing only from April to April, this year's rate of home runs per fly ball is even a little bit higher than it was in 2017.

With that said, the current measurements are no guarantee that 2019 will be another year of record-shattering homer hitting. The trouble with the drag measurements is that they are not consistent from June to August, from week to week, or even sometimes from day to day. Whether because of natural manufacturing variation or differences in the underlying supplies of cowhide and thread that go into the baseballs, drag has a tendency to fluctuate up and down over the course of a year. So the homers that fly in the first week of April wouldn't necessarily clear the fence a week later.

It's possible that this one-week drop in drag coefficient subsides and the baseball returns to its 2018 levels. On the other hand, it's almost equally probable that the ball becomes even more slippery and flies ever farther. Either way, it's clear that the baseball's air resistance is something to keep an eye on for the remainder of the 2019 season. ■

—*Robert Arthur is an author of Baseball Prospectus.*

The Moral Hazard of Playing It Safe

Craig Goldstein

This article originally appeared at Baseball Prospectus on August 6, 2019.

A couple days prior to the trade deadline, amidst a sea of tranquility posing as the lead up to the trade deadline, Bob Nightengale took to Twitter. Nightengale, who was probably wearing his pants backwards at the time, tweeted that MLB GMs were coming around on the idea that the unified trade deadline should be moved back from July 31 to August 15, so they could better assess their positions in the standings and whether they should buy or sell. To which I said:

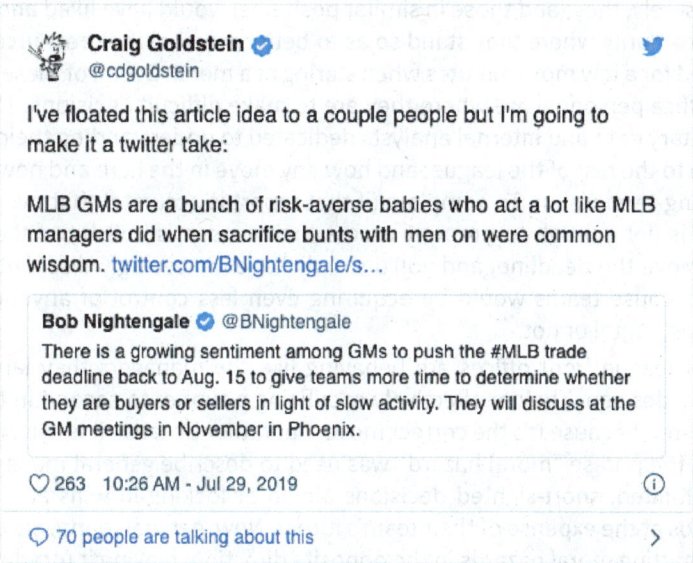

This might strike some as reductive and churlish. And it might be that, but it isn't really wrong, either. Jeff Quinton wrote a great piece discussing the environmental factors that enable front offices to avoid risk without upsetting the apple cart within their own fanbases. I don't believe that it goes far enough, however. His article gives us the proper framework through which to understand why these behaviors have been allowed to seep into front offices throughout the league. Understanding the reasons behind these actions are different from excusing them, though, and GMs should not be let off the hook for their non-competitive approach to the trade deadline (much less the offseason).

⚾ ⚾ ⚾

It's fair to say that fans as a group have rarely, if ever, been pro-player. It is also fair to say that in the time during and following the Moneyball revolution, the pendulum swung from fans who cared intensely about winning in the moment (and thus might be intolerant of a rebuilding approach) to fans who supported building a team that could compete throughout multiple seasons, viewing the playoffs as a crapshoot, with the thought that getting multiple bites at the apple was a better approach than taking a bigger bite in any one season.

There's nothing wrong with that approach, and I still find merit in that argument. However, it seems that the pendulum has swung too far in that direction. Teams are overvaluing some of the individual factors that make themselves long-term contenders rather than attempting to seize a championship when given the opportunity. It's a difficult needle to thread.

And surely, they (and those in similar positions) would have liked another two weeks to clarify where they stand so as to better marshal their resources. We've all asked for a few more minutes when staring at a menu. But all of these GMs and front office personnel are where they are to make difficult decisions. They have proprietary data and internal analysts dedicated to understanding their position relative to the rest of the league, and how any move in the here and now impacts their long-term vision. To complain (if that report is accurate) that over half the season is not enough to properly assess their season is bullshit of the highest order. Move the deadline, and you'd simply have increasingly discounted trade offers because teams would be acquiring even less control of anyone they're acquiring, rental or not.

Major league front offices are behaving like the managers they lampooned two decades ago. They're effectively sacrificing a runner to second in the ninth inning—not because it's the correct move, but rather because it is safe. It used to be that the phrase "moral hazard" was used to describe general managers who made ill-fated, short-sighted decisions aimed at locking in wins and securing their jobs at the expense of their team's future. Now, general managers are guilty of committing moral hazards in the opposite direction, playing it utterly safe and terrified of becoming scapegoats.

In lieu of bold action, they opt to pussyfoot around a current window of contention, choosing instead to play the long game and stack up years of control like they're blocks in a game of Jenga. GMs pass on signing quality players in free agency because the back-end of the deal might look bad, and because they might be able to squeeze out 70 percent of the production from a player who costs a tenth as much. That's a safer investment, too, because it's also hard to prove a negative—it's impossible to prove that Manny Machado would make the Mets a playoff team in 2019-2020, but it's easy to say that the back half of Robinson Cano's contract sucks. Owners, who rule over GM's jobs, are also humans with human brain processes that will always make the so-called albatross contract uglier than the road not taken.

These days, GMs are remembered for the bad deals they make and the surplus value they generate, not the acquisition of expensive, necessary talents that meet their market worth (or fall slightly short while still providing significant on-field value). And front offices know that one or two expensive misfires can cost them their jobs, no matter how many good deals they make.

No front office exemplifies this ethos more than the Toronto Blue Jays. General Manager Ross Atkins had this to say following the Blue Jays underwhelming trade deadline:

This is by no means the first time that an executive will cite years of control to justify their actions, which is often just another way of saying "don't look at what we got, look at how much we got of it." Atkins touts quantity to elide the discussion of quality—either, that of the players acquired, or those given up. Remember: the other teams presumably value years of control, too.

Atkins also had some thoughts to offer regarding free agents back in early 2018:

This ignores, of course, whether the player can create enough value in the front end of a contract to justify the longer term of a deal, and the decline that often occurs in the back end. It also ignores whether the player can fill a need the team requires and put them in a position to compete for and win a championship. But as teams seemingly avoid contention at all, where they might end up having to consider and later justify some of these tough decisions, we still see risk-averse approaches.

Anthony Fenech's article on two trades that recently extended GM Al Avila didn't make got at this issue rather well:

> Passing on those deals was defensible: Both players had yet to break out and trading [Michael] Fulmer—a pitcher who appeared to be a future ace, no matter his injury concerns—would have taken serious gumption, opening Avila up to strong criticism.

Avoiding strong criticism is something each of us can understand as a motivation, but the avoidance of criticism only matters if that criticism is valid. In Fulmer's case, shoving his injury concerns aside affects not only the years that the team controls him (he is currently missing a full season due to Tommy John surgery) but also the quality of those seasons, as his knee and elbow injuries combined to dampen his effectiveness even when healthy enough to pitch. But it was easy to present the then-current image of Fulmer as a top of the rotation pitcher who the team had under its domain for the next five seasons as something to build around. The status quo isn't nearly as often second-guessed as a decision that disrupts it.

⚾ ⚾ ⚾

MLB GMs are risk-averse to a fault. They are ivy-educated and consulting firm-approved, and yet they can't seem to avoid leaving wins on the table in their all-consuming lust for a non-existent $/WAR championship. They are supposed to zig when everyone else zags, and not merely pay lip service to the idea of zigging through a calculated PR plan built on convincing the fan base their approach is novel when it actually apes most of their competitors. Instead they've become far more concerned with making safe, accepted-by-the-new-common-wisdom decisions, such that our prior understanding of what a moral hazard is has become inverted.

I can't blame them entirely, and not only because of the reasons that Quinton illuminated in his article, but also because of the damage wrought by the introduction of the second wild card (WC2) spot. MLB's desire to have more teams in playoff contention has sparked anti-competitive behavior. Teams know now that they do not need to swing big as they assemble their roster because there is a good chance that a mediocre team can either catch fire and capture a division, or muddle along until they back into the WC2.

Simultaneously, the one-game playoff has neutered the WC1, putting an entire season on the flip of a coin like some sort of baseball-obsessed Anton Chigurh. While the one-game playoff makes sense as a way to increase the value of winning a division, it also means that if a front office doesn't like its chances of overcoming a behemoth like the Dodgers or Astros in the offseason, they have few incentives to chase glory. Similarly, the relative inaction in the NL Central at the trade deadline—despite a wide open division—can be explained by the idea that any high-variance investment could still result in only a wild card (or worse) result, given the mere two months left in the season to make an impact.

⚾ ⚾ ⚾

As stated at the top, we should not confuse reasons for excuses. The implementation of the second wild card is just one of many environmental factors that influence how each front office operates. I am convinced that it is one of the larger factors, but I am also convinced that organizations need to shed the yoke of "efficiency at all costs" so that they can instead pursue competition, as the spirit of the game intends. Until they do, we're all deadline losers.

—*Craig Goldstein is an author of Baseball Prospectus.*

Index of Names

Adams, Chance	48	Keller, Brad	58
Arteaga, Humberto	20	Kennedy, Ian	60
Barlow, Scott	50	Kowar, Jackson	93, 104
Blewett, Scott	99	Lee, Khalil	82, 105
Bowlan, Jonathan	90	López, Jorge	64
Bubic, Kris	91, 103	Lopez, Nicky	32
Cancel, Gabriel	98	Lovelady, Richard	62, 112
Candelario, Wilmin	111	Lynch, Daniel	94, 102
Cox, Austin	99, 111	Marsh, Alec	99, 111
Dini, Nick	98	Matias, Seuly	83, 109
Dozier, Hunter	22	McBroom, Ryan	98
Duffy, Danny	52	McCarthy, Kevin	66
Fillmyer, Heath	99	McConnell, Brady	84, 110
Franco, Maikel	24	Mejia, Erick	98
Gallagher, Cam	26	Melendez, MJ	85, 106
Gambrell, Grant	112	Merrifield, Whit	34
Gigliotti, Michael	80, 112	Mondesi, Adalberto	36
Gordon, Alex	28	Montgomery, Mike	68
Greene, Conner	99	Newberry, Jake	70
Griffin, Foster	99	O'Hearn, Ryan	38
Gutierrez, Kelvin	30, 110	Pena, Erick	108
Guzman, Jeison	98	Peralta, Wily	99
Haake, Zach	99, 107	Perez, Salvador	86
Hahn, Jesse	99	Perkins, Blake	87
Heath, Nick	98	Phillips, Brett	40
Hernandez, Arnaldo	99	Pratto, Nick	88, 109
Hernandez, Carlos	92, 108	Rivera, Emmanuel	98
Hicklen, Brewer	98, 113	Rosario, Randy	99
Hill, Tim	54	Rosenthal, Trevor	72
Isbel, Kyle	81, 105	Singer, Brady	95, 102
Junis, Jakob	56	Skoglund, Eric	96

Kansas City Royals 2020

Soler, Jorge 42
Sparkman, Glenn 74
Speier, Gabe 99
Starling, Bubba 44
Staumont, Josh 76
Storen, Drew 99
Tillo, Daniel 97
Viloria, Meibrys 46
Witt Jr., Bobby 89, 101
Woods, Stephen 99
Ynoa, Michael 99
Zimmer, Kyle 78